# ~ THE FAIR SEX ~
# WOMEN AND THE
# GREAT WESTERN
# RAILWAY

## ━ THE FAIR SEX ━
# WOMEN AND THE GREAT WESTERN RAILWAY

ROSA MATHESON

TEMPUS

*Front cover, above:* Women had long been employed in the station refreshment rooms, but during the First World War they were given responsibility for refreshment trolleys out on the platforms as well as serving from wicker baskets hung from round their necks. This poor girl looks somewhat overwhelmed and rather swamped by her uniform.

*Front cover, below:* Once called 'the rail-road', commonly known as 'the track', in railway terminology it is 'the Permanent Way' and maintaining it is a fundamental part of railway operations.

During the Second World War women worked as 'gangers'. The 'look-out' (far right) with armband saying LOOK OUT, flag and whistle is there to keep watch and alert to danger those engaged in oiling the switch blades and locking bars of this point-work. The women are wearing the special 'RAILWAY SERVICE' identity brooch badges on their lapels, which also bore the initials of the GWR on the front and an identity number on the back.

*Frontispiece:* This excellent publicity photograph gives a fantastic insight into the various types and grades of work undertaken by women on the GWR during and after the Second World War. Women such as these played a vital role in the war effort by helping to keep the railways running; without them the railways would have ground to a halt.

First published 2007

Tempus Publishing
Cirencester Road, Chalford,
Stroud, Gloucestershire, GL6 8PE
www.tempus-publishing.com

Tempus Publishing is an imprint of NPI Media Group

© Rosa Matheson, 2007

The right of Rosa Matheson to be identified as the Author
of this work has been asserted in accordance with the
Copyrights, Designs and Patents Act 1988.

British Library Cataloguing in Publication Data.
A catalogue record for this book is available from the British Library.

ISBN 978 0 7524 4419 2

Typesetting and origination by NPI Media Group
Printed in Great Britain

# CONTENTS

*Dedicated to the memory of Mrs Vi Joynes and*
*Mrs Phyllis Saunders and all railwaywomen*

Man's place is not likely to be usurped by *the gentler sex*, whilst man's position may be improved by the judicious use of a class whose services, if employed must necessarily be cheaper, and cannot be competitive.

*The Railway Sheet & Official Gazette*

# Acknowledgements

This book grew out of the research and findings for my doctorate thesis, which itself grew out of the question: 'where are the women in railway history?' Retrospective thanks to the very many individuals and institutions who assisted with information, allowed me access to their resources and gave me railway insight, especially Jack Willcock; John Walter; John Fleetwood; Tim Bryan; Ian Coulson; Phillip Bagwell; Dr A. McMahon; Malcolm Wallis; Prof. Jack Simmons; Swindon Reference Library; STEAM Museum of the GWR; the PRO; the MRC; the Labour History Archive, Manchester; the Railway Studies Centre, Newton Abbot; the Institute of Railways Studies, York and, for their friendship and support, Drs Jill Murdoch and Diane Drummond.

Thanks now to those who – this time around – were at the end of a telephone and shared expertise and also gave valuable assistance: the Revd Canon Brian Arman; Ken Gibbs; Gordon Shurmer; David Hyde; David Colcombe and Adrian Vaughan; also to Peter Rance, Graham Carpenter and Laurence Waters of the Great Western Trust, Didcot Railway Centre, and to Rod Priddle, Peter Sheldon, Eddie Lyons, Lorna Dawes and Elaine Arthurs of STEAM. A particular acknowledgement for use of photographs and assistance goes to Evelyn Cornell and 'Special Collections', University of Leicester Library. My very special appreciation goes to all those railwaywomen and their families who so generously shared their histories, time and photographs with me; without them this work could not have happened. Others who assisted in finding the women: Mike Doubleday; Mrs Betty Griffiths; the Winterton and Swayne families; Roy Newton; Keith Steele; Barbara Dixon; the Institute of Railway Signalling Engineers, Chester Record Office, and helpful local newspapers and journalists around the country for getting my appeals out, particularly Barry Leighton and Gail Middleton.

A huge vote of thanks is owed to Jack Hayward who has acted as an assistant researcher for this book and meticulously 'found' the women in the *GWR Magazine*. Lastly, on behalf of myself and GWR railwaywomen, I would like to thank my publishers for being bold and visionary enough to believe that not just men are interested in railway history, that the part played by women in that history rightly deserves recording and recognition and that it should be brought to a wider readership.

Finally, of course, thanks goes to my lovely family – James, Hanna-Gael, Iainthe and Oona – for kindly support and my husband Ian for holding my hand and helping me 'make it happen'.

*Rosa Matheson, 2007*

# INTRODUCTION

The Great Western Railway Company (GWR) was a grand patriarchal institution that upheld the values of its time. It worked on a hierarchical model. It believed that there was a rank and place for everybody and that everybody should know that place. The world of railways was a masculine world, a world of brain and brawn, of science and technology. It was a place of daring and danger. It was not a place for 'the fair sex' as the GWR liked to refer to women. The GWR wholeheartedly supported *The Railway Sheet and Official Gazette* when it stated: 'The first aim of women's existence is marriage, that accomplished, the next is ordering her home.' Such a stance placed the GWR in something of a dilemma which led to a lifelong problematical relationship with its female employees.

It is in times of crisis and conflict that women as a source of labour come to the fore. The 1870s were critical times for the railways. As a company seeking to minimise its expenditure and maximise its profits, the GWR should have been happy to employ women as they were the cheapest and most suitable labour. This was not the case, not in the offices that is, when this would have brought them into contact with men and lads, a concept that the GWR found 'very objectionable'. After a review in 1876, its superintendents and goods officers felt 'indisposed to the experiment of employing female clerks' despite the fact that women had already been 'Inside' Swindon Works, in a specially created room as part of the trimming shop, for two years. It took almost three more decades before the GWR employed female clerks and then only where they could be kept 'entirely separate from the men'.

Conflict changes many things, often in unexpected ways, and so it was with the two world wars. The First and Second World Wars opened 'windows of opportunity' for women, helping them into the railway offices in larger numbers, whilst also creating new areas of clerical 'female-only' employment. War, despite men's reluctance and resistance, also brought women into workshops, sheds and stations working in wages grades and previous 'men only' jobs. Surprisingly, despite the awful and dreadful nature of the moment, most of the women loved working for the railway and, given the option, many would have loved to stay. Decades later, looking back, they would longingly describe it as 'the best time of my life'.

Many of the girls and women who worked for the GWR were ground-breakers opening the way to railway careers for future generations of working women.

# CHAPTER 1

# THE GWR AND WOMEN

The Great Western Railway, the GWR, or 'God's Wonderful Railway' as many love to call it (but 'God Wot Rot' as it detractors like to mutter), is a name that even today, sixty years after its demise at the end of 1947, is still on everyone's lips. It is a name that still inspires awe and wonder. A name that brings pangs of nostalgia for 'old times'. It is a name that conjures up the magic of the railways. It is also a name, being inextricably linked with the famous Isambard Kingdom Brunel, that evokes quality – quality of achievements, quality of tradesmen, quality of company. It is said that it was Brunel, then a twenty-seven-year-old engineer employed by the company, who gave it the name 'The Great Western Railway', but its vision belonged to four businessmen of Bristol, George Jones, John Harford, Thomas Richard Guppy and William Tohill who resolved to push forward the interest in establishing a railway line between Bristol and London. By January 1833 they had got together a committee of fifteen men, representing the various commercial and corporation interests of Bristol, who agreed to provide funds for a preliminary survey and estimation of the costing for such an undertaking. Brunel was taken on for this purpose. The rest, as they say, is history. The GWR grew into being and, like other railway companies, underwent many heroic struggles for survival. It played a huge role in both world wars and was the only railway company to keep its name and identity after the 'Grouping', which came into operation on 1 January 1923, when some 120-plus separate railways were amalgamated into 'The Big Four'. These were the London, Midland & Scottish Railway (LMS), the London & North Eastern Railway (LNER), the Southern Railway and the GWR. Such was its impact that long after its demise when nationalised on 1 January 1948, people still thought of British Rail Western Region as the Great Western Railway and that they worked for the GWR.

The railways are a masculine world; railways and railway*men* are synonymous. They go together like bacon and eggs, a favourite engine driver's breakfast cooked on the fireman's shovel. Women's entry as paid workers into such a world was never going to be easy. Society, the unions, the men, the companies and especially the GWR were unsympathetic and defensive. Generations of men were born into 'railwayhood'. It is said that GWR's railwaymen were born with GWR stamped on their bottoms. Many women were born into railwayhood, too. They also came from generations of railway families. They worked on the railways and for the GWR. Mrs Nora Hunt was one. She wrote of her family at Swindon Works:

My father became a roof canvaser on coaches and insulated meat wagons … my brother, born 1900, became the youngest foreman in the railway as oil tester and inspector at the oil and grease works… My sister became a clerk in the General Manager's office… I had an uncle who worked in the Brass Foundry… My sister's husband was a fitter and turner … my sister-in-law's husband was a wonderful cabinet maker and wood artist. My contribution came in 1927 when at sixteen I entered the railway company as a shorthand typist in the Chief Accountant's Audit Office. We were a family who helped to run 'God's Wonderful Railway' so that all could share This England.

Despite all this women did not achieve an identity as railwaywomen, certainly during the GWR's time. One has to wonder why? One explanation given to me by a railway*man* is that a railway identity could not be achieved overnight; it came with 'putting in the time' and women's time on the railways had been, overall, temporary in nature, so there was not enough time 'put in'! Another explanation often offered is that women did not come into the railways until the First World War and there were not enough of them to create a collective identity as railwaywomen. This is a widely held but misguided belief as women did work on the railways a long time before the First World War. Whilst it is true the numbers were not vast, they were still significant and still a fact. Edwin Pratt states that at the outbreak of the First World War, the number of women workers employed by the 'whole of the British railway companies' – around 160 at this time, including the GWR

Women had had great difficulty in establishing a 'railway identity'. During the Second World War, however, the GWR, like other railway companies, were happy to promote women's railway and GWR connections. In 1946 several photos and small articles appeared in the *Magazine* under the heading 'Great Western Families'. This is the Loveridge family. The father, Mr H. Loveridge (second from left), was a wagon repairer in the CME's department, Mrs Loveridge and daughter Miss D. Loveridge, both porters, and their four sons, Mr E. and Mr P. Loveridge, firemen, Mr L. Loveridge a signalman and the youngest, Mr A. Loveridge, a messenger. The *Magazine* declared this to be an Oxford record!

Weekly rates of Wages and Hours of Workpeople employed by **Great Western** Railway Company for the first complete week in October, 1886 and 189

The rates and hours should be given for a full week's work, but exclusive of overtime.

| Department, Grade, and Rates of pay per Week. | Number employed. | | Normal weekly hours of labour. | | | | Scale on which overtime is paid. | | |
|---|---|---|---|---|---|---|---|---|---|
| | | | 1886. | | 1891. | | | | |
| | 1886. | 1891. | No. of hours. | Whether inclusive or exclusive of Sunday duty | No. of hours. | Whether inclusive or exclusive of Sunday duty. | 1886. | 1891. | |
| 1 | 2 | 3 | 4 | 5 | 6 | 7 | 8 | 9 | 10 |
| *Each Company must insert the maximum and minimum rates of pay in the blank spaces left for the purpose.* | | | | | | | | | |
| *Ferry Steamer*— | | | | | | | | | |
| Crews of Hoppers and Dredgers— | | | | | | | | | |
| over 30/- and up to ...... | ... | ... | | | | | These men work no Overtime, not perform any Sunday duty | Supplied with full uniform M 1871 | |
| „ 25/- „ „ 30/- | 2 | 2 | 69 | Exclusive | 69 | Exclusive | | | |
| from 20/- „ „ 25/- | 24 | 4 | | | | | | | |
| Carriage and Wagon Examiners and Brake Attendants— | | | | | | | | | |
| over 25/- and up to 30/- | 24 | 36 | | | | | Same rate as Ordinary Time | Same rate as Ordinary Time | |
| over from 20/- „ „ 25/- | 169 | 227 | 60 | Do | 60 | Do | | | |
| from 15/- „ • 20/- | 63 | 52 | | | | | | | |
| Greasers, Carriage Cleaners and Lampmen— | | | | | | | | | |
| over 20/- and up to 25/- | 16 | 14 | | | | | | | |
| „ 15/- „ „ 20/- | 100 | 128 | | | | | | | |
| „ 10/- „ „ 15/- | 46 | 50 | 60 | Do. | 60 | Do | Do. | Do. | |
| from 5/- „ „ 10/- | 100 | 102 | | | | | | | |
| Female Employées— | | | | | | | | | |
| over 20/- and up to 22/- | .. | 1 | Summer Months 10-9 Winter Months 10-6 | Do | Summer Months 10-9 Winter Months 10-6 | Do | Time and Quarter | Time and Quarter | |
| „ 15/- „ „ 20/- | 1 | 2 | | | | | | | |
| from 12/- „ „ 15/- | 60 | 111 | | | | | | | |

Women had worked in Swindon Works since 1874. This 'Return to the Board of Trade' of October 1886 and 1891 shows the numbers employed then, their wages and the differing hours they worked during winter and summer. It is interesting to note the wording at the top, 'Weekly rates of Wages and hours of Work*people* employed…' How wonderfully politically correct it was!

– was 13,046. Most of them were employed in what Pratt described as 'other capacities', such as waitresses, hotel staff, charwomen, washerwomen and waiting-room attendants, all traditional areas for railwaywomen workers. Another little known fact is that the GWR had employed women at Swindon Works decades before 1914, in their trimming shop from the 1870s and the laundry, from the 1890s, as well as in some offices up and down the line from 1906.

The story of GWR and women's employment is like a 'game of two halves', with a different team coming out to play after the break. The first half sees them leaping quickly into action to create employment for young girls in their workshops, admittedly in order to improve their recruitment and retention of skilled male employees, but nevertheless, being decisive, quick and positive. The second half is entirely different. Here we see them passing the ball from pillar to post and asking questions such as: 'what do you think?' 'what do other companies think?' and 'what should we do?' They then went through the process of thinking about it for a very long time, completely losing the ball, before warily deciding to aim at the goal and carry out 'an experiment'! The major factor in this different behaviour is that of class. The GWR were seemingly happy to have working-class women in their workshops, but unhappy about having middle-class women in their offices.

The thinking and implementing of 'the woman question' caused the GWR a great deal of concern and their anxieties did not dissipate once 'the fair sex', as the GWR liked to refer to them, had been established in the offices – in fact the welfare of female employees continued to trouble the GWR throughout its life, particularly in respect of sexual dynamics. Difficulties in

The office photograph! Beautifully composed, elegant and distinguished. Staff in the manager's wages office, Swindon Locomotive Works. Back row, left to right: Miss Gingel; Mr Jones; Mr Poham; Miss Watts. Front row, left to right: Miss Mitcham, Mr Taylor, Miss Budgel. Front centre, sitting: Marion Bruton.

The 'black coat' and 'white blouse' brigade of the signal engineer's office, Reading, 1919. These eight young women are very relaxed in their office wear, their necklines are surprisingly low and their hemlines somewhat high. Compare these to the high collars and ties of the female clerks at Swindon Works – perhaps the Reading ladies have become emboldened by their wartime experiences and working in close proximity to the men. Front row, second left: Enid Davis; fourth left: Gladys Gauntlett; first right: Ella Winterton; fourth right: Elsie Winterton. Second row, first left: Edward Deacon, Elsie's husband-to-be.

relation to this 'very objectionable' situation continued to surface over the decades, even to the extent of affecting working practices and bringing about policy changes. The Staff Committee Minutes during both war periods and women's personal experiences at other times highlight these difficulties. During the First World War, as the number of female employees dramatically increased, 'the female situation' was once again focused upon. Staff Committee Minute No.366 – Women Welfare Representatives – stipulates that it is 'desirable in the larger departments to nominate one woman to exercise general oversight of the female staff'. The focus of this oversight was to be 'in regard to the conditions in which they work, to prevent waste of time in the retiring rooms and to generally ensure that the employment of women shall not give rise to undesirable consequences'. It does not specify what it considers 'undesirable consequences', but it would have related to any kind of contact with the men. In the Second World War these undesirable matters were still on the minds of the Company and to help deal with them a 'Welfare Supervisor for Women and Girls under the Staff and Establishment Officer', namely Miss Emily Brenan, was put in place in 1941. Her job was to deal with 'all matters affecting the welfare of all grades of women and girls throughout the Great Western system'. Miss Brenan was a very qualified and experienced lady. She had graduated from Cambridge University with an Honours Degree in Economics before spending seven years on the staff of the League of Nations at Geneva. During that time she was part of a special research mission under the Rockefeller Foundation and travelled all over the continent and in America. On her return to England she took a post as a divisional welfare supervisor with the LMS which she held for seven years. The *Magazine* notes that: 'Miss Brenan is eminently suited to the important post to which she has been appointed.' Her effectiveness can be seen from the number of times her name crops up in the Staff Committee Minutes, many of which note 'refer to Women's Welfare Officer'.

Miss Emily Brenan was a highly qualified and experienced woman when she took up her post during the Second World War as the women's welfare supervisor 'for all women and girls in all grades'.

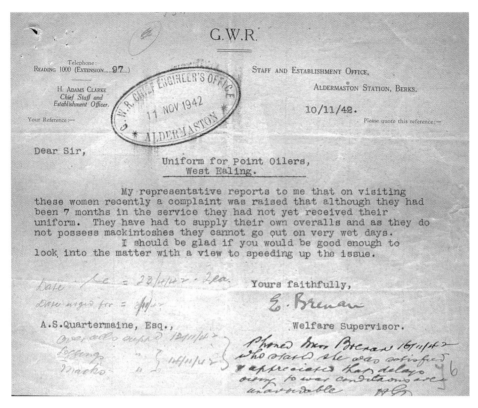

The 'what, when and where' of 'uniforms' was a source of constant discussion and complaints during both wars. Minutes of the Staff Committee Meetings show that a great deal of time was spent talking about and reviewing such matters. In the Second World War much of the problem was tied up in the difficulty of 'clothing coupons' that were negotiable and non-negotiable. Miss Emily Brenan, the newly recruited women's welfare supervisor, had many such complaints to deal with.

One issue frequently raised at these staff committee meetings was regarding the safety of girls or women in respect of the prevention of accidents. Minute SW/1.573/6(b) makes amusing reading highlighting as it does, the stereotypical thinking of the times:

Miss Brenan reported that it had come to her notice there was the mistaken belief on the part of some of those responsible for the engagement of women employees that heavily built young women were necessarily best suited for manual work. This is not the case and the fact should be borne in mind by all concerned, having regard to the risk of an individual sustaining injury in attempting to lift weights beyond her capabilities.

Another area concerning the 'safety' of the women raising sexual tensions was in respect of their being on their own with the men on night shifts. Minute SW/1,573/8(a) records the Company's anxieties:

… local officers should be required to exercise discretion in regard to the utilisation of women under the age of twenty (particularly those under the age of eighteen) so as to avoid, as far as possible, their employment on night work, especially when they would not be accompanied by other women on such duty.

Mrs Enid Saunders, then single and in her twenties, remembers such an incident:

> This particular night no girl called in and I was there all night on my own with the men. Mr Shackles came up to me and said 'You're here all on your own young lady, are you nervous of the men? Would you like another girl to come over?' and I said 'No, they're all perfect gentlemen, they don't harm me, they help me, help me with everything, and there's no problem.'

The Company's concerns regarding women's welfare could even change accepted working practices. This happened in the Swindon Works Telephone and Telegraph Exchange in the early 1920s. Mrs Vera Radway, then Vera Reeve, a young girl aged just sixteen years, still very a much a junior in terms of work experience and status, was rostered to work alone in the Exchange on a Sunday. This was standard practice until one day Mr Kelynack, the chief clerk, entered and asked to see 'the person in charge'. 'I am,' replied Vera. 'Don't talk like that Miss Reeve. Don't talk like that,' Mr Kelynack said. 'Well, I must be,' she responded. 'I'm the only one here.' 'We can't have that,' he said 'I'll have that stopped.' So the policy and practice were changed. After that, there were always two women rostered for work on a Sunday, a junior and a senior. This story was known of, and related to me, by several others who had worked in the Exchange at the time or a little later. When Vera was asked if she thought it was because Mr Kelynack did not think a junior would be capable enough, she replied: 'Oh no, he didn't think it was safe – safe for a girl or woman on her own, with the men coming round you see.' When asked: 'Did men come to the office often then?' Vera replied, 'No, hardly ever. They didn't have any need to come round there, except the night staff – two of them and they were disabled.' Here we can clearly see that, for the Company, the 'woman problem' was still problematic. Women were supposed to be cheaper labour, yet here, because of the Company's supposed concerns for their physical and moral welfare (although, no doubt, also wanting to ensure that business was being conducted properly by an appropriate person of appropriate status) they were costing the Company money, having to now pay for the two – rather than the one – on a Sunday shift. On this evidence it could be argued that the GWR took their responsibilities towards women employees very seriously, no matter the situation or circumstance.

War is a 'circumstance' that figures large in respect to women and the GWR; in fact war is a recurring theme, necessarily so as it played such a large role in shaping the working lives of railwaywomen. The twentieth century was shaped by war. It was, indeed, the first century of what historian Arthur Marwick calls 'total warfare'. Total warfare required the participation of previously under-represented groups such as older women and housewives and even young children, who became 'essential players' rather than 'sideline onlookers', when they found themselves part of the new and eventually conscripted workforce. In these times, the railways, too, became part of this new conscription. O.S. Nock described them as 'the weapon for total war'.

During the two world wars all women became more visible. They could be seen to be occupying work and public places in which they previously had no presence. The war years, although small in number, were massive in their impact on a catastrophic worldwide scale. Yet it is true that whilst war wrecks, plunders and destroys, it also creates, transforms and reconstructs, thus presenting life-changing opportunities in the face of adversity. It can be said, and many will argue its cause, that war created a 'window of opportunity' for women that altered their lives – sometimes beyond recognition – and in so doing restructured their social status and identity. The call to war work was a welcome release for many women in both periods. They exchanged

One way women did their bit for the war effort was by transferring their 'womanly' skills of cleaning to carriage cleaning, thereby releasing men for Service.

menial tasks, isolation, little or no free time, low wages and subservience for dangerous or demanding, yet seemingly exciting and patriotic work, with social camaraderie and a relatively high wage, as well a certain amount of independence. Women who worked on the railways during the wars experienced huge changes that 'turned their lives upside down' in both work and home terms and yet this time was described by most of the women interviewed as 'the best time of my life'. Little wonder as, for the first time, women were praised and valued in 'male terms'. Press and propaganda cried: 'She's a real woman doing a man's job.' Women were suddenly seen as adults. They had, to quote Collie Know, 'put away childish things and proceeded to astonish the world'. Such a quote highlights society's thinking regarding women.

In both wars the vocabulary used to entice women into the workplace was couched in patriotic and heroic terms. They were encouraged to think of themselves as 'doing their bit for their country'. Mrs Joy Stone (*née* Handford) was one of those women 'who did their bit'. During the Second World War she was secretary to 13th Battalion (GWR) Home Guard at their headquarters at 3 Emlyn Square. She had been seconded from the CME's office for the duration. Joy remembers being on standby for the telephone on D-Day. Should the invasion have gone wrong, a codeword from Salisbury Plain District would have come through to GWR's Home Guard alerting them into action. In the evenings and weekends Joy was voluntarily in charge of the Swindon Girls Training Corps preparing and supporting young girls aged between fourteen

Members of the Swindon Girls Training Corps during the war, leaving Swindon station for the journey to London where they took part in the National Youth Rally of 1946. Front row, left to right: Officer Commanding Miss Joy Handford; Cadet Diane Rew; Officer Cadet Pamela Taplin; Cadet Jean Hooper; Cadet R. Brown; -?-. Back row, left to right: Cadet Audrey Sharland; Cadet Valerie Collet; Cadet M. Hazell. All but Miss Taplin worked for the GWR. What a happy bunch they are.

Policewomen on parade at the GWR Home Guard and Civil Defence Units gathering at Castle Bar Park in 1943. Nearly 1,000 members of GWR's staff took part. (Courtesy of the University of Leicester)

and eighteen years of age, who wanted to enter the Women's Services, until they were old enough to enlist. It was almost a GWR section as 99 per cent of the girls worked in the GWR offices.

In both wars the Government urged the women to come out of their homes and into the workplace, but, both times, the companies and the men were far more reticent to welcome them, especially railway companies and railwaymen. During the First World War the GWR were not alone in their reluctance to take on women workers. Edwin Pratt writes that as late as August 1916 returns to the Railway Executive Committee from sixty-eight railway companies showed that some companies 'were still employing no women at all, [whilst] others had not increased their number during the war'. The First World War made incessant demands for men to join the armed services and women were desperately needed to replace them in order for the railways to continue to operate and play their part in the war effort. The Government put increasing pressure on the railway companies to take on women. Mr Frank Potter, the GWR general manager, who was a supporter of the recruitment of women, reported to the Board on 23 April 1915:

> As a further means of releasing men for service with the Colours, the extension of the employment of women is in process. For sometime past it has been the practice to employ women clerks in general offices and goods offices, and their services are now being utilised as booking and parcels clerks, also as ticket collectors, dining-car attendants, etc.

If we look at the total numbers of women and girls employed by all the railways in all capacities during the course of the war we find the following figures:

| Date | Year | Number of Women Working on the Railways |
| --- | --- | --- |
| August 4 | 1914 | 13,046 |
| December 31 | 1916 | 46,316 |
| December 31 | 1917 | 65,389 |
| September 30 | 1918 | 68,801 (the maximum) |
| October 31 | 1918 | 68,637 |

Source: Edwin Pratt, *British Railways and the Great War*, 1921

On 4 August 1914 the GWR had employed a total of 1,371 women and girls – 497 on railway work proper and 874 in other capacities. The 497 included 278 who were engaged on clerical duties – mainly typists, shorthand writers, telegraphists and telephone operators. The remaining 219 have not been identified anywhere. By March 1917 the GWR numbers stood at 5,000 and in March 1918 at 6,174. At this time the Midland Railway were employing nearly 9,000 and the North Eastern Railway, who had employed 1,575 before the war, now had 8,520 including 1,052 in the shell shops.

The Railway Institutions struggled to come to terms with female labour on the railways and sought to contain the women whilst protecting railwaymen's interests. The Railway Press were quick to air their concerns and add to the debate about the 'unsuitability' or 'limitedness' of women, voicing the misgivings and inner feelings felt by the railway men. In August 1915 *The Railway Gazette* wrote:

> That the employment of women on the railways of this country has contributed in no small degree to the maintenance of an efficient transport service cannot be gainsaid. ... Female

*Above:* Already waitresses in the refreshment rooms, the First World War saw women being employed as stewardesses on the trains too. She stands at the door of Dining Car No. 9545, while the trains waits at platform No.2 at Paddington station in 1917.

*Right:* By working on the railway women, such as this booking clerk, 'did their bit for their country' during the First World War. (The *GWR Magazine*, 1917)

labour, however, is limited to those grades in which experience is not of the essence ... and the vocations must not entail contact with train movement.

By the end of October 1916, however, returns to the REC from twelve of the 'leading companies' showed that between them they now employed over 33,000 women and girls 'in no fewer that 135 separate and distinct occupations'. Those numerically identified are:

| Occupation | Number in Employment |
| --- | --- |
| Clerks | 13,904 |
| Carriage-cleaners | 2,173 |
| Workshop women (various) | 1,278 |
| Platform porters | 1,098 |
| Goods porters | 901 |
| Ticket-collectors | 706 |
| Gatekeepers | 705 |
| Engine-cleaners | 587 |
| Labourers | 239 |
| Machinists | 178 |
| Parcel porters | 147 |
| Messengers | 150 |
| Horse-cloth & sack repairers | 121 |
| Painters | 99 |
| Number-takers | 79 |
| Cellar & page girls | 40 |
| Weighing-machine attendants | 23 |
| Brass lacquerers | 23 |
| Letter-sorters | 15 |
| Horse-keepers | 14 |
| Carters | 12 |
| Train-attendants | 11 |
| Cloakroom-attendants | 10 |
| Luggage-room porters | 10 |
| Wagon-repairers | 8 |
| Hotel porters | 6 |
| Harness cleaners | 6 |
| Train information attendants | 4 |
| Crockery collectors | 4 |
| Ferry attendants | 2 |
| Bridge-keepers | 2 |
| Blind pullers | 2 |
| Wharfingers & flag maker | 2 |
| Gardener | 1 |
| Carver | 1 |
| Printer | 1 |
| Signal cleaner | 1 |

Source: Edwin Pratt, *British Railways and the Great War*, 1921.

*Right:* Carefully posed photographs of 'feminine' female clerks such as these in the district goods manager's office at Worcester appeared in the *GWR Magazine* and reassured male readers and male employees that, despite entering a 'man's world', the girls remained entirely 'womanly' and no threat to men's jobs and livelihoods.

*Below:* This delightful photograph of clerks, tracers and draughtswomen of the signals drawing office, Reading, in 1918, did not actually appear in the magazine. Perhaps it was just a little too alluring or whimsical.Left to right: Elsie Winterton, Ella Winterton, Gladys Gauntlett, -?-, Enid Davis, -?-, -?-.

The inter-war period saw many women and girls being retained in the offices as well as traditional areas of women's railway employment. A Census of Staff for the week ending 9 March 1929 shows that just over ten years after the First World War the GWR employed a total of 3,357 women and 163 girls in 1928, but 3,309 women and 113 girls in 1929. The figures for 1928 show that there were a total of 1,865 female clerical workers, 146 in shops and 1,411 identified in other roles.[2]

During the First World War the GWR had been reluctant initially to expend the effort, time and money to improve circumstances in order to accommodate female employees at a time when the Company was already hard pressed. In the Second World War the Company was just as resistant to female employees and no less pressed. In *The Great Western at War*, Tim Bryan says:

> Ultimately it was only the employment of women which would really make an impression on the severe [staff] shortages faced by the Great Western. However, as usual, it seems that the Company and its staff, not always renowned for their progressive attitude, were slow to embrace the opportunities presented by the availability of female staff.

Indeed, once again, the unions and men displayed strong opposition towards the employment of women in railway work, not only at the commencement but throughout the Second World War. This time it was Ernest Bevin, the Minister of Labour, who had to work to bring together the employers and the unions involved to secure their cooperation. Under the terms of the agreement reached, the demarcation between men's and women's work was eliminated for the duration of the war. However, it was strictly understood by all that women were to be regarded as purely temporary workers and allowed to do men's work only to the end of the war. This agreement was incorporated into the Restoration of Pre-War Practices Act 1942, which gave it the full force of law. Talking about this and women's response to it, Mrs Vi Joynes explained: 'We all knew it was only for the war. We had to do our bit though, didn't we?' This time around the Government and the railway industry were more prepared for a war emergency situation. For a start, there were fewer companies to deal with as most had been amalgamated into The Big Four. The mobilisation of female labour was more organized, more intensive and with much larger numbers recruited into a wider range of jobs and grades. Prior to the Second World War around 26,000 women were employed on the railways; the greater proportion being engaged in clerical work with the remainder being employed in the domestic category. A list compiled by the GWR in September 1941 – which identifies the areas in which they had taken on women in the place of men – shows the inroads women had made into different categories and men-only jobs. Under 'Conciliation Grades' it lists fourteen occupations including: engine cleaner, oiler, tube cleaner, stores issuer, shed labourer, and electric truck driver. Even more are identified under the heading 'Shop Etc., Staff' which identifies forty-eight different occupations: acetylene cutter, drop stamper, electric welder, electric plater, electrician's assistant, hammer driver, carriage fitter and rivett hotter are amongst them. The final heading 'Miscellaneous' identifies three occupations as lift attendant, messenger and telephone attendant. There are a total of sixty-five different capacities, other than clerks or domestic, in which women were employed on the GWR.

In Swindon Works the women were employed in a number of different workshops. They were often moved around, switching between railway work and sometimes, as in the First World War, on what they called 'war work' such as munitions. In the First World War 'munitionettes' skin often turned yellow. In the Second World War it was other skin complaints that a number of women mentioned – mainly dermatitis – as Mrs Alice Coale found:

War brought unusual work opportunities to women. A female billboard poster attaches an advert for Brylcreem – the then essential hair product that made any man 'cool' – to the cast-iron gates on Platform 7 of Paddington station.

Female train announcers were a daring innovation in the Second World War. Like their male counterparts they would have undergone careful voice tests before being appointed to address the public. Each item of 'authentic information' had to be introduced by the phrase: 'Train announcer speaking' and delivered 'slowly and carefully'. So successful did the women prove that a small article in the *Daily Herald* (March 1946) stated: 'Women Train Announcers Stay. The forty women train announcers recruited by the GWR during the war are to be retained.'

Railway factory workshops made ideal 'temporary munitions works'. During both world wars the GWR was commissioned to produce munitions and weaponry and this was carried out in Swindon Works; both times, women 'dilutees' were taken on for this.

We did all this! Women line up with job description cards for a public relations photograph. This was just a small selection of hundreds of different jobs actually carried out by women during the Second World War. The King Class locomotive behind the women, rigged with blackout tarpaulin, looks as if it could benefit from the attentions of the female engine cleaner on the far right of the picture!

I first worked in B Shop varnishing shell cases. I got dermatitis from it. We had to varnish lots of shells all day. At the end of the day we used paraffin to get the varnish off our hands. After working there for a while I came out all in spots, all over my hands and up my arms. I went to the doctor's and he said it was something in the paraffin that didn't agree with me. I was off work on the club for three weeks. I had dermatitis off and on for years after that ... had to go into hospital once because it was all over me. Dr Bennet said I could go back to the factory, but not to the same shop.

The Second World War was the time when women were said to have flooded the railway offices. An article in the *Daily Telegraph* (August 1941) reported: 'Rail Clerks Call-up: 30,000 jobs will have to be taken over by women.' This was the beginning of what was to become known as the feminisation of railway offices, when women came, they saw and they stayed. Previous practices and policies were pushed aside or forgotten, some never to return. Married women, even with family responsibilities, were required to stay in work. Ex-employees, who had left once married, such as Mrs Elsie Deacon, a draughtswoman at Reading, were recruited back, alongside the new single young recruits. It all shows how desperate the country and the Company were to maintain the workforce. This desperation to get more women into the offices was to completely change the course of office life for the future.

A booklet produced by the British Railways Press Office in 1943 records that: 'spread throughout Britain there are 544,715 railwaymen and 105,703 railwaywomen'. Details in *The Railwaywomen's Annual* (1949) showed that by the end of the war women had worked in 'nearly 250 different railway grades'. Quite an accomplishment! One way or another throughout the war women showed they could make the grade, as the Queen acknowledged in her speech to the women at the end of the war. It was, she said, 'a difficult job magnificently done.' In 1945 the war ended and just a few months later in 1946 the GWR reprinted an article from *The South Wales Weekly Argus* of Newport, Monmouthshire, recording thanks and paying tribute to 'the Great Western railwaywomen' employed at Newport and up and down the GWR system. The country and the companies were signalling the women, 'the war is over, it is time to say good-bye.'

## South Wales Thanks the Women

The *South Wales Weekly Argus*, Newport (Mon.), has recently published the following tribute to the work of Great Western railwaywomen during and since the recent war :—

For nearly seven years, 37 different jobs—from plate-laying to train announcing—have been undertaken by women at Newport and other stations on the Great Western Railway.

Now, with the gradual return of ex-servicemen to their former jobs, the numbers employed are being reduced. Passengers will miss their cheery and efficient work in all branches. Their work was not only concerned with the goods and traffic department, but with the signal, locomotive and engineering departments, too.

About sixty women have been employed at Newport, and they have shown remarkable versatility and willingness to perform jobs which, before the war, were done by men. The travelling public have grown accustomed to women passenger guards, ticket collectors, announcers, porters and enquiry clerks. Unusual jobs successfully tackled were

those of motor-van drivers and signalwomen, while one took charge of a horse-drawn delivery van.

Less in the public eye, but achieving considerable success, were women who took over the work of booking and goods clerks, engine and carriage cleaners, fitters' and boiler-smiths' mates, and general labourers. Others became proficient in assembling and dismantling automatic instruments and telephone maintenance work.

Platelaying, bridge and office painting, involving work on scaffolding and on the permanent way, were readily undertaken.

During the war a trained team from Newport Goods Department entered a railway fire-fighting competition at Bristol and, though they did not win, they proved they would have been very valuable had they been called upon to extinguish a fire.

Now the majority are returning to their homes, but their work will always be remembered as being performed with zeal and efficiency—and always cheerfully.

In 1946 a great many women were still in the railway offices. Possibly realising that this was the office of the future, the GWR set up a Training School for Girls at Paddington. In 1947 an article entitled 'They Learn as They Earn' was published informing the reader that the trainees who came straight from school, were given 'special aids and considerations which are best calculated to initiate them easily and pleasantly into business life … and the art of life'. After passing a 'simple education test' to see if they would profit from such tuition, the fifty to sixty girls underwent further general education and shorthand and typing instruction. They received full rates of pay, although technically only working half a day. When they successfully qualified as shorthand typists they would enter into 'full-time Company service'. With forty having already qualified, the Company was pleased with the school's success. Whilst the majority of women left the workshops, stations and sheds almost immediately, and were happy to do so, staffing shortages continued for a number of years and in 1947 – for what was to be the GWR's last year – a limited number of women were still employed in men's jobs. They did not last much longer though, and neither did the GWR. On 1 January 1948 nationalisation of the railways became effective and the Great Western Railway Co. ceased to exist.

1   Figures taken from *The Railway Gazette*, March 1918, p. 369.
2   GWR Census. David Hyde Collection.

The Great Western Training School for Girls at Paddington. The morning session in the Great Western classroom; these girls are entering business life in the most sensible way.

# CHAPTER 2

# WOMEN IN THE WORKS

Swindon Works was, to quote Mrs Vera Radway, 'a world within a world'. Known locally as 'Inside', it was a bastion of masculinity: fundamentally and essentially male. In male eyes and, it is true to say, in most female eyes also, women had no place there. Yet it is inside Swindon Works that the GWR first employed women. Actually, it was not quite 'Inside' but in a workshop at the edge of the Works that bordered the railway village.

By the 1870s Swindon Works was well established. Over the decades it had had its ups and downs and in the 1870s the factory found it difficult to recruit skilled men. The reason for this was, according to Mr Holden, superintendent of the Carriage Department, that: 'Men had refused to come to Swindon because there was no employment for their daughters … unless a man sent his daughters out from home there [was] nothing for them to do.'

Mr Joseph Armstrong, the then manager of the Works, a 'Company man' but known to be straight and fair and considerate towards his workforce, had 'long been anxious about the employment of girls in New Swindon' and had decided that the Company needed to take action in order to resolve what could become a serious problem. Mr Armstrong decided the Company would need to assist in finding work for them. As with everything, the GWR preferred to do this in-house. In March 1874, at the joyful celebration to mark the completion of the first Royal Saloon, Mr Holden had more good news to announce. Such was the regard that Mr Armstrong had for the welfare of his men, he said that 'it was intended to find employment for the girls in the upholstery department of the Carriage Works'. He was 'glad to say they were now fitting up a separate shop for girls [which] would have a separate entrance and be kept entirely distinct from the men. Every provision would be made for their comfort.' It was hoped that 'bye-the-bye shops would be specially erected for them and they would be enabled to employ large numbers of girls'. This announcement, reported in the *Swindon Advertiser*, was received by hearty cheers from the attending railwaymen.

Swindon Works drawing No.1633, dated 1872, shows that there was an extension of the carriage paint shop and a new trimming shop, and drawing No.2329, dated 1876, shows a further extension to the carriage work and an added mess room. These shops bordered London Street. The new trimming shop was the area in which the women were placed. This can be substantiated from these drawings and from a description carried in a book published in 1892: 'Through another range of carriage shops, we enter the trimming department. Here the upholstery of the carriages is looked after. This we find is the only department in the Works in which women are engaged.'

An official Swindon Works register of workmen shows that three short months after the March announcement women started working 'Inside'.

## Alphabetical Register of Workmen Carriage Dept: Oct 1877–1907

| Name | Entered | Left | Job |
|---|---|---|---|
| 1874 | | | |
| Mary Burge | 15/8/74 | 13/11/80 | Ling Wm |
| Cecilia Fullond★ | 18/7/74 | | POL |
| Mary Isles | 15/8/74 | 13/11/80 | POL |
| Jessie McGregor | 15/8/74 | 24/12/78 | POL |
| Martha Ribson | 15/12/74 | 23/12/80 | POL |
| 1875 | | | |
| Caroline Shaw | 3/11/75 | 1/7/87 | POL |
| Isabella Turnbull | 23/6/75 | | POL |
| Sarah Jane Sanders | 16/7/75 | 10/10/78 | POL |
| Harriet Smith | 16/7/75 | 5/4/78 | POL |
| Rachel Smith | 13/8/75 | 12/4//90 | POL |
| Ellen Dempsey | 2/11/75 | | POL |
| 1876 | | | |
| Eliza Brown | 4/9/76 | 17/7/79 | Ling Wm |
| Mary Ann Johnson | 25/1/76 | 23/2/76 | Ling Wm |
| Eliza Jess | 16/11/76 | 26/3/79 | POL |
| Sarah Princk | 26/2/76 | 13/8/80 | POL |
| Eliza Smith | 22/2/76 | 18/6/78 | POL |
| Emma Saunders | 14/11/76 | 24/1/78 | Ling Wm |
| Mary Watts | 29/3/76 | | POL |
| 1877 | | | |
| Mary Jane Adams | 9/8/77 | 16/8/78 | POL |
| Matilda Brettle | 28/11/77 | 9/5/81 | POL |
| Eliza Dent | 26/2/77 | 19/7/82 | POL |
| Annie Ellerington | 21/11/77 | 28/3/79 | POL |
| Mary Fisher | 20/9//77 | | POL |
| Eliza Greenman | 8/10/77 | | Ling Wm |
| Emma Jane Hyde | 18/8/77 | | POL |
| Eliza Longman | 19/12/77 | 27/9/81 | Ling Wm |
| Ellen Maisey | 12/11/77 | 27/9/80 | POL |
| Mary Morgan | 9/8/77 | 15/7/81 | POL |
| Elizabeth Pavey | 28/8/77 | 25/6/78 | POL |
| Jane Pinnett | 31/7/77 | 26/9/79 | Ling Wm |
| Mary Price | 24/9/77 | 16/1/82 | POL |
| Sarah Ann Roderick | 28/11/77 | 3/7/78 | POL |
| Etty Smith | 18/7/77 | 3/9/78 | POL |
| Maud Margaret Townsend | 1/5/77 | 3/9/78 | POL |

1878

| | | | |
|---|---|---|---|
| Sarah Butcher | 14/1/78 | | Ling Wm |
| Laura Louisa Bramwell | 8/10/78 | 11/6/80 | POL |
| Emily Clapham | 13/2/78 | 5/11/80 | POL |
| Emily Clarke | 11/3/78 | 10/4/79 | POL |
| Mary Ann Dawe | 27/5/78 | 1/7/78 | POL |
| Eliza Mary Hall | 21/1/78 | 24/7/78 | Ling Wm |
| Mary Jane Hoskham | 28/1/78 | 3/5/78 | POL |
| Eliza Hall | 16/12/78 | 23/6/81 | Ling Wm |
| Elizabeth Howard | 9/9/78 | ------ | POL |
| Florence Holliday | 17/9/78 | 7/7/82 | POL |
| Elizabeth Ellene Jefferies | 13/2/78 | 27/3/78 | POL |
| Mary Poynter | 8/10/78 | 27/8/80 | POL |
| Emily Jane Taylor | 21/10/78 | 9/12/78 | POL |
| 1879 | | | |
| Emily Martha Hale | 17/11/79 | ---- | Ling Wm |
| Eliza Little | 24/11/79 | ----- | POL |
| Jane Morse | 30/4/79 | 8/8/79 | POL |

The register claims to be alphabetical, but does not appear to stick too rigidly to this description. A Miss Celia Fullond, marked with ★, appears to be the first woman to be employed in a GWR workshop and is recorded as commencing work on 18 July 1874 as a polisher. The job description of the women is either that of polisher or lining women, later known as sewers. Out of the first five, only one is sewing. What is surprising is that initially more women are employed as polishers than as sewers. Polishing, as in French polishing, was a skilled trade. It seems highly unlikely that initially the Company would have happily invested the time or manpower in training these young women for such craft positions, knowing that their employment was just a short-term measure before marriage, It would appear, however, that the women quickly proved capable at polishing and it is known for a fact that at least from 1892, women did do French polishing and the GWR continued employing female French polishers in a separate workshop right up to 1947.

A Company Return submitted to the Board of Trade for 1886 and 1891 identifies that in 1886 there were sixty-one female employees at the Swindon Works, whilst in 1891 this number had risen to 114, a not insignificant number. An 1892 booklet, *The Great Western Railway, The Town and Works of Swindon*, confirms this and gives us a little more information:

About 100 in all are employed; some French Polishing; others working sewing machines, making nets and various other descriptions of work in connection with the carriage trimming. The arrangement for the comfort of the women appears to be carefully studied. They are provided with a separate entrance and leave at somewhat different hours from the men.

The tradition of taking on the daughters of the workmen in these shops, persisted throughout the GWR's life. Even as late as 1946 it was known as accepted practice. Mrs Kath Grayhurst, whose stepfather Art Grey was an electro-plater in 15 Shop, remembers: 'I went into McKilroy's restaurant when I was fourteen and then Garrards, but I was just waiting till I was sixteen to go Inside. I knew I would because that's what always happened when your father was in there. I knew I would be a polisher.' Interestingly, Kath was probably amongst the last female polishers taken on by the GWR before it was nationalised. Describing her job Kath simply says: 'It was a hard job. Heavy work.' In 1942, under the heading of 'Applying the Shine' the *Magazine* offers

## TEA AND ENTERTAINMENT.

The annual gathering of the females employed in the G.W.R Works Carriage Department, and their friends, was held on January 6th, in the Mechanics' Institute, New Swindon. About 250 sat down to tea, provided by Mr. Blatchley, manager of the G.W.R. Coffee Tavern. The tables were presided over by the following ladies :—Mrs. Turner, Misses Long, Deasey, Barnett, Oakley, Burns, Hole, Barker, Jones, and Davidson. The hall was beautifully decorated with flags, &c. After the tea the hall was speedily arranged for an entertainment, in which the Zingara choir took a successful part ; also a song and dance by Misses G. Workman and R. Rollins, which was prettily rendered and encored. Songs of a more humorous character were given by Mr. Harvie, the respected foreman, which greatly added to the success of the evening, and was repeatedly encored ; a comic duet, " Money matters," by Misses Workman and Boyce, was also greatly applauded. The choir was beautifully arranged by Miss Workman. The programme was as follows :—Chorus, " The merry Zingara," the Choir ; song (encored), " Miller and Maid," Miss Workman ; duet (encored), " Blue Alsatian Mountains," Misses Lovelock and Russell ; song, " While the silver," Miss Boyce ; song (encored), " Willie, such a tease," Miss Sheldon ; recitation, " Faithful unto death," Miss Rollins ; pianoforte duet, " Not love," Misses Workman and Hedges ; song, " The little kitten," Miss G. Workman ; comic duet, " Money Matters " (encored) " Two cousins," Misses Workman and Boyce ; song and dance, Misses Workman and Rollins ; duet, " Convent Bells," Misses Rebbeck and Williams ; duet, " Larboard watch," Misses Rebbeck and Esau ; humorous songs, Mr. W. Harvie. After the above a sketch was given, entitled, " The wishing gate," the leading characters being taken by Miss Workman as Kathleen ; T. Noddy, her lover, as a soldier ; also a Fairy Prince, by Miss Boyce ; the Witch, Miss Higgs, and the Fairy, Miss G. Workman. All characters were taken in a creditable manner. The rest of the evening was enjoyed in dancing, which closed at eleven o'clock. Mr. G. Workman was conductor of an efficient string band.

*Above:* French polishing was a skilled trade usually designated as a man's job, yet from the time women went into Swindon Works in 1874 they were employed as polishers and officially identified as French polishers in 1892. The GWR created this workshop solely for female employees. There were separate shops for male French polishers as well. The GWR continued to employ female French polishers right up to its demise in 1947.

*Left:* Tea and Entertainment: Whilst the men's departments held annual *dinners*, the women had *tea*. As well as food there were entertainments organised and put on by the workers themselves.

this description: 'A job universally regarded as mysterious and difficult. The job, whilst certainly highly specialized, is one quite capable of being mastered, given practice and patience. The work is carried out in several stages and the professional evinces a certain fastidiousness in his attention to detail.' The article points out that there are three workrooms in the polishing section of Swindon Works, one of which is staffed by women – so in 1946 little had changed.

The *Census of Carriage & Wagon Works and Timber Stores Swindon Actual Number of Men on Register 4 weeks Ending May 20 1944* identifies that in 10A Shop, there were thirty-three female polishers. This shop, amongst several others, came under the collective responsibility of Foreman H.S.L. Barrat. Inside 10A Shop would have been a female forewoman and female charge-hand. Kath remembers in her time there a Miss Woodruff, the forewoman, and Vi Newton, the charge-hand. Kath's work day started at 7.30 a.m. She would put her metal check with her works number on to the board and put on the pinny she supplied herself, then find the gauntlet gloves provided for her. Her job was to polish anything that was made of wood in the train – doors, panels, window frames, luggage-rack poles, wood partitions, even toilet seats. The women were trained up by the charge-hand, 'and you were expected to learn fast,' says Kath:

> You were hard at it all the time and there was strictly no talking. You even had to ask the charge-hand to 'be excused' (i.e. go to the toilet). It was always the charge-hand we spoke to. We hardly ever spoke to the forewoman, and certainly not in a familiar way. She was a lot older than the rest of us but it just wasn't done. She ruled with an iron rod. Very strict. There was a big distance between her and the rest of us.
>
> The workday varied as the work was brought in daily, depending on what was needed. Working on a door would take about five days with other bits of jobs in between.
>
> First you had to lift up the door and place it on your bench, then you had to 'pickle it' that is, take off all the old polish and strip it down to the wood. This would take about a day. It was horribly messy. We had to wear gauntlet gloves that went right up our arms for the stripping as it was very dirty work. The special stripper we used was really sticky, like mud. Then came the 'filling-in' with wood filler to make good any damage. After that it had to be completely sanded down with coarse sandpaper. Next came the colouring – or toning – to bring up the wood and the grain. Different colours would be used for different wood effects (the article identifies that walnut, mahogany, oak and birch are used for coachwork and furniture) This was done with a camel hair brush and a special liquid. You had to really work it in, then it was sanded down again but using a much finer grade sandpaper, known as flour. Next you had to brush polish the wood. When it was dry you lightly sanded down again. Lastly it was 'padded out', that is polished and buffed up with special cotton pads and methylated spirit. This could take anything up to two days depending on the weather and conditions inside the workshop. If it had been polished one day and then been very cold overnight, a 'bloom' would settle on it. To remove this bloom and get it back to a shine meant a great deal of hard rubbing and buffing. Lastly it had to be 'passed' by the charge-hand. If it didn't come up to standard you were in trouble as it had to be sanded down and then padded out all over again.

In 1874 the comfort of the women who would be working in this shop had been forefronted by Mr Holden in his announcement that 'every provision would be made for their comfort'. It is also specifically mentioned again in the 1892 booklet: 'the arrangement for the comfort of the women appears to be carefully studied,' but in the two years she worked there Kath remembers little comfort or amenities:

> The shop was very drab. It was grubby and chilly. We had our own large bench to work at. There were no seats. The windows, along the outside wall, were too high up to see out of.

There was an urn of hot water for making tea which we used to make by using a double-sided spoon with holes in. We brought in our own condensed milk.

Other comforts consisted of a washroom with two basins, one toilet but no mirror. Kath remembers that a special kind of pink soap/disinfectant was provided for washing their hands and to wash off at the end of the shift. The polish and muck would harden during the day making it really difficult to get off. The women found cleaning with meths (methylated spirits) was best, but even so, a lot of hardened stuff was left behind which had to be picked off at home. All of this was not kind to the skin and Kath developed dermatitis which was an ongoing and common problem. There was also a mess room under the workshop. Here there was a gas ring with a kettle, an old Belfast sink and a few tables and hard chairs. 'Not many people used it,' says Kath, 'it was very cold and dim, but if you came in from the country as I did, there was nowhere else to go for the lunch hour. Money was tight, so it was not much good going up Regent Street to the shops.' Even taking into account that this was the early post-war period, it would appear that the GWR had lost their scruples regarding the female workers' need for comfort as it had obviously lost significance. Kath did not stay long at GWR, leaving in 1949 to get married; however, she was lucky because she was one of the few women who left with a trade and with a reputation of having had good GWR training. French polishing in those days was in great demand and Kath was even headhunted by local a firm, Gilberts, to work for them.

In 1946 the female polishing shop was overseen by a forewoman assisted by a female charge-hand, but with a male boss above them. Records show that in 1890 and until at least 1894 this male boss was Foreman Mr W. Harvie, who was probably assisted in a matronly, if not charge-hand manner, by a Mrs Turner. We learn of Mr Harvie through the reports of the 'annual tea of the female staff employed in the Carriage Department', in the *Temperance Union and Great Western Magazine*. The report of 1890 records that it is the third such event held in the hall of the Mechanics' Institute with 'an excellent tea provided by the GWR Coffee Tavern Co.' There are reports for five consecutive years. They are written up in some detail: 'a song and a dance by Misses G. Workman and R. Rollins, which was prettily rendered and encored' or 'the choruses were sung by the young ladies … attired in pretty gypsy dresses'. It is recorded that each annual event is presided over by a Mrs Turner and members of the committee. Whilst Mrs Turner is at every event, the younger committee women change over the years. In 1890 it is just Misses Deasy, E. Belsher and Poolman, whilst in 1894 it is Misses Long, Deasy, Barnett, Oakley, Burns, Hole, Barker, Jones and Davidson. In 1890 nearly 100 ladies sat down to eat, but in 1894 it was a significantly larger 250, presumably by this time they are entertaining family and friends. Once the tea is over the real fun began. The tables were moved, the floor cleared and an evening of entertainments of some sophistication commenced. Music and song very quickly became embedded in New Swindon's culture and every opportunity was taken to perform and to appreciate it. In 1890 there was a concert, in 1892 there a dramatic performance entitled *Zilloh, the Gipsy Queen* and in 1894 there was an entertainment evening made up of solos, duets, a recitation, a song and dance and a sketch entitled *The Wishing Gate*. Every year there were also a couple of 'humorous songs' by Mr Harvie which are said to 'greatly add to the success of the evening'. Each year finished with dancing to a band and, before the evening ended at 11 p.m., Mr Harvie – variously described as, 'the popular foreman', or 'the respected foreman' – always 'complimented the ladies upon the great success of the tea and entertainment'. In 1892 he surpassed himself, commenting that 'he was surprised and pleased that the ladies were so clever as to get up such an excellent dramatic performance'. The females of the Carriage Department were obviously very talented ladies. It would have been nice to hear more of their doings over the years but, somewhat perplexingly, after these five reports this item disappears from the magazine, although reports of other annual dinners and other departmental gatherings are still recorded.

*Right:* Mrs Kath Grayhurst knew she would get a job in Swindon Works because of her family connections. Kath left school at fourteen and 'killed time' until she went 'Inside' aged sixteen in 1946 to work as a French polisher. It was hard, dirty work in miserable surroundings, she remembers, but she left with a trade and was headhunted by a local furniture firm to work for them.

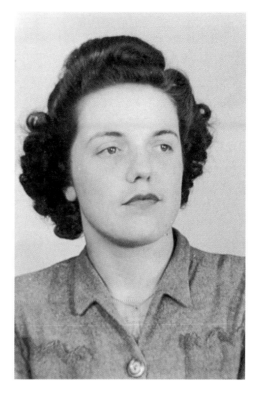

*Below:* There were 832 knots in the diamond-shaped netting of a compartment luggage rack. It required eighty-one yards of material and about one hour to make. The nets in the third-class compartments were made of hemp which came from Italy, but those in the first-class were made of artificial silk and in the 1930s were in the Company's colours of chocolate and cream. Originally the nets were made in-house by women in Swindon Works sewing room, but by the 1930s the work was outsourced, the third class going to the Institute of the Blind to which these two young women belonged.

Whilst they may have started with the daughters, the GWR later developed a tradition of also employing the widows of their male employees in many different capacities – crossing keepers, tea ladies, in the stores, and as clerks – all around the system, but particularly in the trimming and polishing shop. It became accepted knowledge amongst the women of Swindon that when your husband died you could apply to the Company for employment. Mrs Kath Salter remembers this most clearly because of her Aunty Amy:

She went to work Inside when Grandmother was a widow. You had to be a widow or an orphan to go Inside... 'cos I used to say 'when Dad dies I'm going to work with Aunty Amy'. I think she would have been eighteen or nineteen. It must have been about 1917/18, she was in there in the First World War, the Great War ... 'cos she used to knockabout with a war widow ... the war widows used to get in there as well you see.

My Aunty Amy worked down the swimming baths at first. She had to go in and see that the little cubicles were alright and clean and once some man had left his false eye on the shelf. She worked for the Great Western for quite a while because she didn't get married until quite late... nearly 40 I think.

She used to work in the sewing shop. She was there in that photo with Queen Mary [1924]. I remember that because I went up with the school to wave to her. She [the Queen] didn't say nothing, just walked round. She was very austere wasn't she. That's is how they were brought up

Women in the sewing room of the trimming shop at Swindon Works. In the mid-1870s the Works was finding it hard to recruit suitable men. The men did not want to come to Swindon because there was no employment for their daughters. This shop was specially created to offer employment to them and resolve the problem. This created a tradition that lasted until 1947.

*Above:* King George V and Queen Mary made a Royal tour of Swindon Works on 28 April 1924. The Queen visited the Sewing Room and can be seen watching girls making the netting for the carriage luggage racks. Behind the Queen is the CME, C.B. Collett, and then the King. Mrs Kath Salter remembers that her aunt who worked in the shop was unimpressed by the Queen: 'She was very austere and didn't say nothing!'

*Right:* Mrs Ivy Wilson, on the left wearing her Uncle Bill's tin helmet and tunic, worked as a fitter on munitions in Swindon workshops during the Second World War. Her sister Joan Edmonds, wearing Bill's army cap, worked in the trimming department. She liked working on the sewing machines best.

to act. Aunty used to make the netting for the luggage but that wasn't actually her job, because she used to do the sewing, you know towels and all that because they used to make everything in the Great Western. She used to have to go on polishing. She didn't like that French Polishing. That was hard work she said. Then sometimes the laundry. She wasn't very keen on that and then this netting, but she liked the sewing machine the best. She had done some work down the shirt factory before she got in there because she had to wait for a vacancy. It was something wonderful if you did get in there. She liked it there, but she wanted to leave to get married. There was quite a lot of women in the shops when Aunty was there.

Women were still in the trimming/sewing shops decades later during the Second World War, and one who also liked the sewing the best was Clive Wilson's Aunty Joan. Her father, Frank Edmonds, three of her brothers and her two sisters all worked for GWR. Alice, the eldest, worked in the laundry and Ivy went into the machine shop during the war. It would appear that the practice of moving the women around between the various jobs within the trimming shop still continued, because Joan 'worked on everything' says Clive, 'but it was the sewing machine work that she enjoyed the most. She would cut to measure and sew all the roller towels for the toilets, make the head covers for the seats or the curtains for the trains.' Once Joan worked on a special job making the curtains for the royal train. All the women learnt about upholstery, making the covers for the seating. 'Aunty always said you could tell which class of coach they were working on, first or not, because of the quality of the material being used,' remembers Clive.

Despite Mr Armstrong's hopes and good intentions; apart from the addition of the laundry in 1893, which then provided jobs for around ten more women as laundresses, but which eventually grew to over fifty laundresses in the new purpose-built laundry; women made no further progress into the workshops proper until the First World War.

# CHAPTER 3

# TELEGRAPH AND TELEPHONE OFFICES

Whilst the GWR had made their way by being bold and daring, even risk-takers – they had, after all, taken on an extremely young and somewhat untried engineer to build their railway – they had always maintained a traditionally conservative attitude towards their workforce, particularly in areas related to skill. In the nineteenth and early twentieth centuries it was accepted belief in society that only men could perform skilled work but also that not all men could be skilled workers. The GWR kept strict control over who could and could not become 'a skilled man'. The GWR tradition insisted that only skilled men's sons could follow them into skilled jobs. Sons whose fathers were in unskilled positions had to tolerate this thoroughly unfair practice and accept the position the Company decided they could have, or look for a job elsewhere. The GWR considered the notion of women working in skilled jobs to be untenable. They ignored evidence revealing any aptitude shown for such work and they continually ducked or bypassed the issue. The subject of women telegraph and telephone operators is such an area.

The GWR were the first railway company to really see the potential of the telegraph for the railways, indeed they had it installed as early as 1838. Afterwards in 1910 they modestly wrote: 'it needed no great foresight to perceive that the telegraph and telephone would become such important factors in the conduct of railway work.' The telegraph was a new work opportunity for aspiring young men, much as when computers were in their infancy. The Post Office, however, had quickly taken on female telegraph operators, finding them to be more suitable for their requirements. They had found women were better than men in several respects. The women had 'a good eye and ear and a delicacy of touch'. Particularly appealing was the fact that, overall, the women were more malleable and less complaining and a whole lot cheaper, 'requiring very few salary increments because they left to get married'.[1] Some railway companies had quickly followed suit but it was not until 1908 that the GWR bit the bullet. In 1909 an article in the *Magazine* gives good insight to this story in respect of Company thinking and attitudes, as well as general business practice in the country. It is fun to see that the GWR actually had to admit not only that women had proved themselves capable but also that they were 'admirably suited for telephone and telegraph work'. It writes:

> About thirty years ago the General Manager of the GWR suggested the feasibility of employing women operators in the more important telegraph offices on the system. But the idea was not then carried out. Since that time, however, women have demonstrated their possession of ability

to succeed in various fields of labour although up to the present their employment in railway work, especially in the south, has been comparatively limited.

Having set the scene and acknowledged that women are working for notable companies and other railways, the GWR announces, in an upbeat though serious manner, that it has decided to join in:

> The GWR has recently introduced women into the telegraph and telephone operative section, thirteen learners and a supervisor having started at Paddington and six learners and a senior operator at Bristol. At the latter a new office has been provided with adequate accommodation for both male and female staff, whilst at Paddington structural alterations necessitated by the innovation are now in progress, and when completed, will result in the provision of an up-to-date and well equipped operating room.

It is obvious that by this time the GWR have realised that this type of 'worker' may be the way of the future. Its rivals have tried and tested them and found them a useful investment, still, the GWR needs to reassure its shareholders that this is not a fanciful 'flash-in-the-pan' notion but an investment in the Company's future economic prosperity. It seeks to reassure them that the matter has been thought through and a strategy put in place for progressing things as quickly as possible to get full value for their expenditure in new facilities and new employees:

> In order to train the operators, a School of Telegraphy has been temporarily established at Paddington so that when the office is ready the whole of the operators now in training may be competent to carry on the work required of them. Until recently learners had not been scientifically trained as, after passing the examination, candidates were drafted to a convenient telegraph office to learn the work. In some cases they laboured under difficulties, and, although they were supervised by a competent clerk, the same facilities for learning were not to be obtained so conveniently in an ordinary telegraph office as in a properly equipped school with a qualified teacher. In the new school, sounder and single needle circuits have been erected, … and as soon as the learners have mastered the alphabet they are given actual messages to signal under the rules and regulations obtaining in a telegraph office.

As if all this was not enough, the GWR then announced it had employed a *lady* supervisor at Paddington who had 'considerable experience of railway telegraph work', which 'augurs well for future success'. So pleased were they with the whole idea that the GWR included a photograph of the 'new school' with its nine female pupils sat at desks, staring at the camera. It is extraordinary that the GWR, who resisted employing women in such situations so strongly and for so long, then announced to the world that the success of their telegraphic and telephonic operations rested in the hands of a 'lady'. All of this would have raised grave concerns in respect of men's employment and job security so at the end of the article the Company put this matter firmly to the forefront:

> It is generally known that the duties of a telegraph operator are arduous and exacting, but there is no reason to suppose that the ladies will be found wanting, and it will then be possible for the male operators to be drafted into positions where there is greater scope for obtaining promotion in the service.

Finally, should the ladies be patting themselves on the back too enthusiastically, it adds a splash of cold caution with a very pointed word – 'experiment'. 'The *experiment* will be watched with interest, and will, it is hoped, meet with success.' So began a new era in the GWR's relationship with female employees, and a new sphere of employment for women, which was eventually to become a 'woman-only' area in the GWR, at least during the daytime, and was to persist throughout the life of the GWR, and after!

Whilst we do not learn of the identity of the 'lady supervisor' when her arrival is announced, we do learn of it when she left in 1915. That she made her mark in terms of impact on the programme and on the people is obvious from the unashamedly enthusiastic and high praise showered on her in the *Magazine*:

> Just over six years ago the first female telegraph operators were put into training at Paddington, and since that time Miss Hamilton... has with marked ability acted as supervisor. From the commencement her task was no sinecure, as she first had to take in hand and train raw hands, most of whom had never seen a telegraph instrument, to become expert operators. Tact, patience, energy and discretion were qualities which were indispensable for such a position, and Miss Hamilton possessed them in a marked degree.

The GWR had chosen well in their person to lead their experiment and Miss Hamilton had not let the women's side down. The women too must have proved their worth because female telegraphers became part of the GWR permanent work force and were soon being employed up and down the system. The article also states that at Bristol a new office specifically for this purpose will provide 'adequate accommodation for both male and female staff' whilst at Paddington 'structural alterations necessitated by the innovation are now in progress'. A 1910 photograph in the *Magazine* of a view of the new main telegraph office, Paddington, shows a largish room with six rows of long benches with four stations at each. At least ten women are apparent sitting alongside male operatives under the regulation of a standing male and female supervisor.

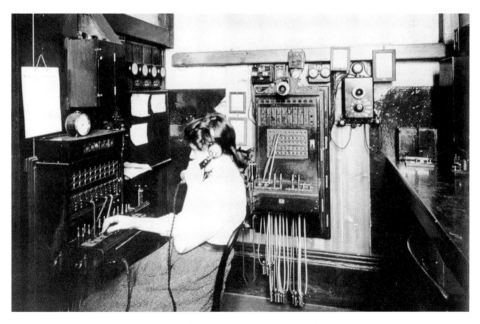

A splendid picture showing an array of different telephone and telegraph communication systems. On the extreme right can be seen the electric telegraph tapper which required the user to have a knowledge of Morse code.

From the *Magazine* we learn a little of the work histories of some of these newly trained, pioneering telegraphists. Miss Mary Caldwell became the chief supervisor of the Paddington telegraph office in 1915 and remained in the post for eleven years before returning home to Scotland. Mary was not only good at her work, she was also good with her staff for the article tells us: 'She had endeared herself to the staff under her control, and in every possible way had taken a keen interest in their welfare. Her leaving was a source of great regret among her friends.' Sadly, sometimes we only learn about their lives by reading about their deaths:

Mrs Nellie Gwendoline Slocombe (*née* Shaw) passed away on 7 November 1918 and Miss Ellen Louisa Hazell on 24 October 1918. Mrs Slocombe joined the National Telephone Co. in 1908 as an operator, and was transferred to the GWR on 9 February 1912. She was a skilful operator, and her charming character endeared her to all. The tragedy of her death was enhanced by the fact that she was first employed as a telegraph operator. She was subsequently transferred to the telephone room, and was an operator of sterling worth. Two deaths coming with such tragic suddenness naturally cast a gloom over the telegraph and telephone staff, and the deepest sympathy of all was expressed to the relatives.

The death of Elsie Moody at Swindon Works Telephone and Telegraph Exchange, who died of pneumonia following influenza in October 1918, and that of Elsie Annie Lewis, who joined the Paddington telegraph office in 1909 (she must have been one of the original intake) and who went on to become assistant supervisor, are also reported. Elsie 'passed away on 4 February 1919, after an illness of only a few days'. The winter of 1918/1919 was the time of the Spanish influenza pandemic which killed many thousands across Europe. For some reason the GWR's telephone and telegraph female operatives seemed particularly vulnerable and several deaths, up and down the line, are

*Left:* This well-known photograph of a GWR telephonist and telephone exchange in 1910 has a special elegance and composure about it that is lacking in many others showing the telephone systems and exchanges.

*Opposite:* Paddington's telephone exchange during the 1930s employed around fourteen operators and two supervisors. It would have been a very busy job handling the incoming and outgoing calls from the general public and GWR's own departments. It looks very stark and regimented.

reported. More happily we learn of Miss N.I. Griffith as she left to be married in 1919. We are told: 'Miss Griffiths joined the GWR at Paddington on 3 October 1910 and within a few months was transferred to Birmingham, where she was the first female telegraph operator there.'

The National Telephone Co. were also quick to take on women as telephone operators. They found that the women had a better manner with the customers than the men and generally coped better with the job. In July 1906 'a private branch telephone exchange' in the Great Western Hotel, Paddington, was opened by the National Telephone Co. with its own female operators. The GWR were very enthusiastic stating that 'the advantage of such a complete and up-to-date installation cannot be overestimated', adding: 'needless to say that the management staff have found the telephone exceedingly useful'. Telephony was seen as a great advance over the telegraph as it did not require such extensive training and there was no need to master intricacies such as the double or single-needle or Morse code. By 1910 the GWR's own local exchange switchboard at Paddington had the capacity for 100 lines and trunk calls could also reach Slough, Windsor, Reading and Swindon. The usefulness of the telephone had not always been apparent to all those who worked for the GWR as is noted in a 1913 article in the *Magazine*. Under the title 'Great Western Telephones Paddington' the GWR is enthusing about its spanking new telephone system, designed in-house by the signal engineer. It was multiple-type, with 1,000 extension lines, seven stations for female telephone operators and a switchboard, which is 'believed to be the largest railway switchboard in the kingdom'. It pointedly remarks: 'The reluctance with which, until quite recently, the installation of a telephone was accepted, was difficult to account for' especially when after it has 'fought its way into acceptance' and been in use sometime, 'even the merest suggestion of withdrawal is met with voluminous objections' but now 'little remains of the former prejudice'.

The former prejudice against women as telegraph or telephone operators was also abating and the numbers employed continued to grow. The Census of Staff for March 1914 shows that

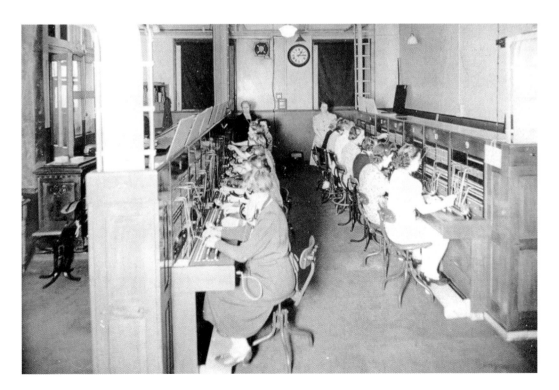

By the mid-1930s the teleprinter was superseding the telegraph. It was considered a tremendously useful innovation as one did not need specialist skills such as working the single needle or double needle, or knowledge of Morse code. Anyone who could type and count could use the teleprinter. All telegrams were coded. 'XP' was very important, 'SP' was next in importance and they were also time coded. 'A' was one o'clock and 'B' was two o'clock. All words sent and received were counted and noted down.

the GWR employed fifty female telegraph and telephone operators, four female supervisors and seven girl 'learners' in their passenger (later known as traffic) department.[2] It was not too long before telephone operator or telephonist became synonymous with female and GWR's telephone work eventually became the domain of women, apart from the senior supervisory roles and night shifts. In their magazine pages the GWR often describes these operatives as 'telephone clerks', although they did little or no traditional clerical work.

The telephone and telegraph offices at Swindon Works, which had at one time been scattered around the offices and station, eventually, unlike that at Paddington, were combined into one 'exchange'. Circular No.2243 dated February 1913 identifies an office called the 'Central Telephone Exchange'. *The GWR Register of Female Clerks* shows that 'telephone and telegraph learners' were taken on early in 1912. Doris May Towell and Elsie May Callandine were employed in January and Ethel Barnett, Flora Porter and Winifred Pauline Johnson followed in March. After four weeks training they were classed as qualified operators and had an increase of wages from 4s to 6s a week. From 1919, during the day, the Exchange was an all-female environment, under a female supervisor. It was an entirely separate space and, to use the words of Mrs Vera Radway who worked there in the 1920s and 1930s, 'once inside the door one would not see another person apart from those with whom one was working. You were confined to barracks.' Indeed many women interviewed who had worked there between the 1920s and 1947 found this very irksome and rather claustrophobic. Mrs Radway did not like this enclosed separation:

> I didn't like it at all being inside all the time. I should have liked to have gone out and mixed with other people... walk around the corridors and seen some different people to speak to. When you get the same people amongst you all the time... it can get a bit boring. I would have loved to have gone into another office to work, for a change, but once you were there, that was it.

Mrs Violet Lane (*née* Peaple) also felt this:

> We always felt isolated. You were all girls and you were shut in. No one ever came into the offices to see us. The only way we could recognise anyone was by their voice, we knew voices very well. When you were walking down the tunnel, or in the street, and you would hear a voice, you would think 'Oh, that's Mr so-and-so,' but if you met him face-to-face you wouldn't know who he was until he spoke!

In Swindon, the new juniors were 'trained up' by the more senior members on duty at the time. There was a great deal to learn so it took some time, as one had to learn both telegraph and telephone systems. One had to master the Morse code; learn by heart the telegraph code call signs for all the different stations up and down the line; memorise the hundreds of individual extension numbers on the switchboard for Swindon Works as well as numerous well-used external telephone numbers and those that were in constant use, such as Paddington and Bristol offices. 'You also had to have a good knowledge of the GWR system, where signal boxes and stations were,' said Violet Lane. 'Knowledge in itself was not sufficient, one had to be speedy in thought and quick of hand; all this before even going near one of the machines.' This 'learning on the job', doing it the GWR way, was a much prized element in the cultural make-up of a GWR man, and it held true for those women who had worked in the Telephone Exchange too. The women of the Exchange, like the trained men, knew that the GWR reputation would open doors to other workplaces too. One woman remembered she had had no trouble later getting a job with the Post Office as a telephonist. 'They knew I came from the GWR and so I would have been thoroughly trained and could speak properly.' Speaking clearly and with proper pronunciation was a requisite element of the job. Vera Radway remembered. 'You really had to be very right in everything you did. You had to speak properly. You had to speak clearly and be understood because it wasn't everyone who was used to using telephones then and they could be put off just by a simple point, then everything could go wrong.' Another important aspect of the job was the ability to spell correctly. Once thought competent enough to cope with using this knowledge and with using the machines, the women would take 'turnaround sessions' in either the telephone room or the telegraph room (these were separated by a short passageway) during their shift. One of the reasons for this was that the machinery, i.e. the telephone switchboard, and headphones were cumbersome and heavy: 'It made my head ache,' said Mrs Kitty Webb. 'It was so noisy and heavy.' Violet Lane remembers one switchboard being very 'arm aching'. As well as all this the rooms, which were small, were often very warm, even extremely hot in the summer. 'We would swish the skirts of our dresses to try to make some cool air around us,' remembers Violet. 'It was difficult because we couldn't just get up and walk around.'

Whilst there was plenty of incentive to 'get on the machines and do the job' at the beginning of their working lives, once on the machines there was little other career progression, just the

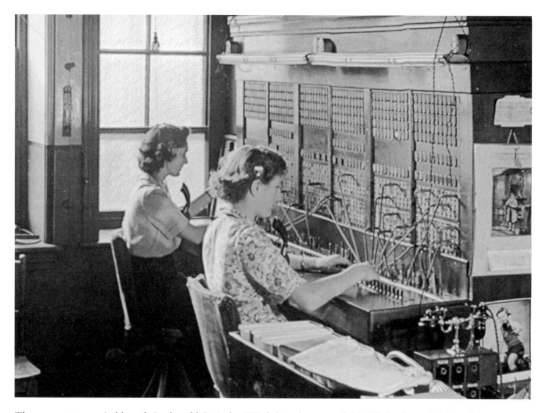

There were two switchboards in the old Swindon Works' Exchange and Mrs Violet Lane (*née* Peaple) and Peggy Wallis, on the right, sit at the Works' internal switchboard, which had hundreds of different numbers. This board was called the 'doll's-eye' board by the girls as when the number indicator dropped down, it looked a bit like a doll's eye.

increments in salary that came according to age and the seniority of time. There was only need for one supervisor and for one supervisor's assistant. Miss E. Gutteridge, and Miss A. Retter both joined the GWR on 1 January 1912. Miss Gutteridge became a telegram and telegraph learner in the Engineer's Office at 4s a week whilst Miss Retter was taken on in the same capacity in the Loco. & Carriage Dept. On 15 January 1912 Miss Retter became a qualified operator at 8s a week whilst Miss Gutteridge was promoted to supervisor in the Loco. & Carriage Dept at 16s a week. Some five years later on 1 August 1919 Miss Gutteridge became the supervisor of the telephone and telegraph office with a pay increase to 40s a week . She remained the supervisor up until the demise of the GWR and for sometime after. Miss Retter became the assistant supervisor in May 1929, a position she retained until her retirement in 1950.[3] The only other seniority available to the women was gained through time on the job and taking responsibility as tutors for training up the juniors. This frustrated a lot of the women who worked there over the years. Violet talked of her own frustration: 'You just had to wait hoping one of them would leave or retire – or something! I remember feeling very restless and applying for posts outside.' Many would have liked the opportunity afforded to the male employees of being 'freed-up' for obtaining promotion elsewhere in the service.

Although this position was classified as clerical and the women talked of 'working in the office' it is clear from the way that they spoke that they thought of themselves as telephonists/

Left to right: Beryl Morse, Elizabeth Smith and Pat Chapman (*née* Turner). All calls, internal or external, had to be connected by the Works' operators. They had also had to deal with trunk line calls, Post Office lines and signal omnibus lines.

telegraphers rather than as clerks. Their work carried with it a huge sense of responsibility. Upon them depended the safety of the railways; of railway workers, passengers, commercial products and railway stock. Vera Radway recalls that when commencing their employment they had to sign an agreement to never leave their post, even in wartime and never to strike. She remembers during the 1926 General Strike: 'We weren't allowed to strike. I just had to go in. It was understood by everyone that we had to.' During the war the telegraph offices were responsible for giving the colour-coded alerts and air-raid warnings along the line, however, the women at Swindon Works, like those in the Telephone Enquiry Bureau in Paddington, were expected to remain at their posts whilst others were evacuated to the safety of the air-raid shelters. Violet recalls: 'we gave the air-raid warnings, but we were not allowed to go out to take refuge. We had to stay there.'

The GWR were continuously improving their telephone systems as the volume of work through this increased. At times it was obvious that the volume of use was outstripping the capability of the system to handle it and that calls needed better management. In 1921 it wrote an article laying out specific instructions of what to do and what not to do when using the telephone. It lays down four rules: 'Always listen before ringing; Give prompt attention to calls; Announce who you are; Be brief.' It reminds them that three people are involved in making a call, the caller, the called and the operator, and that all must cooperate for a successful call to be

Betty Carter and Violet Lane (*née* Peaple). Violet sits at the dial station. There were no dialling facilities at this time (*c.*1940s) and this had to be done by the Works' operators.

made. It informs that there is no need to shout down the telephone and instructs that one should say 'goodbye' at the end of the call to indicate to all that the call is finished, thereby assisting the operator in clearing the line. It stresses that whilst it is not saying 'all operators are angels … they are generally expert at their work', indicating that most of the problems experienced lay elsewhere. Women who worked at the Swindon Exchange in the 1930s and 1940s, however, confessed that:

> … on some occasions we would cut people off, especially if they had been rude or were talking for too long and holding up the line. It was not done often but we couldn't have people holding on, so we had to try to keep the conversation short. Everything was checked by the clock you see, we had to note the time the call started and when the call finished so either way someone was likely to get cross with you.[4]

Another area of telephonic work that became a predominantly female environment (the male supervisor aside) was the Central Enquiry Bureau at Paddington. The GWR had an enquiries counter on Paddington station during the First World War. So useful did this become that in 1928 they set up a Central Enquiries Bureau dealing with telephone and postal enquires in the office of Superintendent of the Line. The hours the telephones were answered grew from nine hours to fifteen hours a day and to seven days a week. In 1932 it became part of the in-house Publicity Department. This also began a time of changing personnel from seven men in 1932 to fourteen women, including an assistant supervisor in 1938, and up to twenty women and three female assistants when Miss Davenport took over in 1939. The staff on telephone enquiries needed a wide range of geographical and railway knowledge and they were trained, in-house, on a course lasting between three to four months. The enquiries received did not just relate to the times, routes, departure platforms of the train or cost of tickets, but a mixed bag of allsorts from the practical – 'what is the weather forecast?'

From the late 1930s the office of the telephone central enquiry office became an all-female domain with a female supervisor and assistant supervisor. The women operators needed an extensive knowledge on a wide variety of matters, not always railway related, and had to undertake a four-month in-house training course before being allowed to answer enquiries. (Photograph courtesy of the University of Leicester)

to the sublime – 'who am I?' from one unfortunate gentleman who frequently forgot who he was and where he lived, but could find his way to the enquiries counter on the station. During the war there were extra difficulties to deal with, along with the staff shortages and increased numbers of enquiries there was the need to keep one's gas mask and steel helmet hanging from one's chair and the constant interruptions of air raids. The Bureau rose to every challenge and held a special 'claim to fame' – at no time during the war did the Central Enquiry Bureau cease to operate – and their course of action during the raids became legendary throughout the system:

> Each girls curls up on her little enquiry mat in the kneehole space under her desk, perches her telephone on a half pulled-out drawer and just carries on with her service that is a blend of accurate knowledge, patience, tact, courtesy and the 'smile in the voice'.

It would appear that the women who 'manned' the Enquiry Office were made of sterling stuff, for when they made it onto the pages of the *Magazine* their praises and achievements were sung loud and clear. In 1946, a whole page article entitled 'Wisdom While You Wait' in the *Magazine* tells the story of three learned ladies to whom 'Bradshaw (the railways timetable) was an open book', Miss N.E. Smith, Mrs E. Lachner and Miss K.S. McKay:

> These three London girls, now well known to thousands of railway passengers, were among the pioneers who helped to prick the bubble of masculine superiority in the timetable world.

How Paddington telephone central enquiry office coped with telephone enquiries during air-raid alerts in the Second World War became legendary in their own time. (Photograph courtesy of the University of Leicester)

[They] started a partnership in 1916 in the enquiry office at Paddington, which has only just ended with their retirement. Together their careers with the Company total more that a century of service. They made many personal friends by their courtesy and won much favourable comment for the Company by their competence.

The article gives information regarding their 'run-of-the-mill' work - 'boat and bus connections, inter-availability of tickets, road, rail and river trips, circular tours, and excursions', along with amusing anecdotes of their 'out-of-the-ordinary work', such as 'The case of the frightened seaman', and coping with 'a wild-looking man with a revolver'. In more serious form it tells how the women worked shifts to cover the office all through the Second World War, 'even whilst the Nazis showered death on London', and comments on their courage to which Mrs Lachner responds: 'We weren't doing anything out of the way – nothing at all to make a fuss about. It was the job and it had to be done.' The article finishes in warm, complimentary fashion:

The three 'learned ladies' now step down from their counter assured of their place in the rich tapestry of the Company's history. They will be happy in the knowledge that the younger generation, whom they helped to train, will be carrying on the exacting task in the true 'Lachner, Smith, McKay' tradition.

If the GWR believed that these women deserved to be recognised in their history, then so do I! Miss M.C. Steward, supervisor of the Telephone Exchange Paddington and Miss Davenport, clerk-in-charge of the Central Telephone Enquiry Bureau, were rather notable too in that they both received the British Empire Medal (Civil Division) for their dedication to duty in extremely difficult circumstances; Miss Steward was decorated in the King's Birthday Honours List of 1945, and Miss Davenport in the New Year's Honours List of 1946. The *Magazine* tells us that Miss Steward had held her position for over eight years and had skilfully trained her twenty-four women operators to cope with the 12,000 plus calls a day. She had, it writes, sustained the efficiency of the Exchange all through the heavy bombing because of her 'complete command of the situation in all emergencies and the high sense of duty which she had herself displayed and inspired in others'. Miss Davenport, who had been in post since 1939, also receives high praise. Throughout the war she had 'discharged her duties with the highest efficiency', which included training-up all the new staff – taking them through the four-month course. She kept the office operating despite all difficulties and her staff handled over 7 million public enquiries during the war. On top of this she also achieved five certificates in station accountancy, railway signalling and railway law.

The women that worked in GWR's Telegraph and Telephone offices were, undoubtedly, women with 'something about them'. They delivered a first-class service despite the numerous trials and tribulations they faced over the years. The physical apartness from the other office workers, being in separate offices, heightened their feeling of being something different to other clerks. Conversely working for the GWR also made them feel 'very special'. It was this label or identity of being something 'special' that came with working for the GWR which attracted many of the women to the job.

1   Jane Lewis, p.197.
2   Staff Census 1914. David Hyde collection.
3   Information from Staff Records, Local History Archive, Trowbridge Reference Library.
4   All information on Swindon office taken from Doctorate Thesis, interviews and *GWR Magazine.*

# CHAPTER 4

# THE OFFICES

In the late nineteenth century, for a variety of reasons too numerous to go into here, many middle-class women needed to find paid employment. The expanding world of the office and the rise of the clerk and the typewriter, offered new possibilities to them. The employment of women in railway offices greatly troubled the Railway Press. *The Railway Sheet & Official Gazette* offered words of caution and advice: 'The bulk of the fair sex are averse to the mastery of intricate details and would be unable to stand the strain demanded by the office work of the railway service.'

As more railway companies were dipping-their-toes-in-the-water to test the idea, *The Railway Sheet*, in January 1877, again raises the matter. It writes:

> The fact of female labour becoming an element of our railway offices is now and again suggested by the Press; and only last week it was stated that the experiment had been tried and was about to be extended. The Metropolitan, it was said, had so employed female clerks, and the Great Western were about to follow suit. As a matter of fact, the Metropolitan have done nothing of the kind and the Great Western are merely considering the question.

They were right. The Great Western had been 'considering' the question of women clerical workers for over six months. An extract from the minutes of the meeting of the Board of Directors at Paddington dated 16 August 1876 indicates that: 'It having been stated that some Railway Companies had tried the experiment of employment of women in some of their Offices with good results it was ordered that further enquiry be made upon the subject with a view to its future consideration by the Board'.[1]

The response from the Great Western superintendents to this enquiry was surprisingly quick, just two weeks later, and surprisingly positive. They state:

> It was the opinion of this meeting that female clerks might be employed with advantage, but their employment should be confined to offices (such as Goods or Abstract offices) where they could be employed separately from the men clerks, except when the member of a station master's family might be employed at the same station as himself.[2]

It all appears very promising – until further investigation. A further letter from the superintendents is worth printing in full as it gives insight not only into the thinking and rationalisation of the GWR officers, but also the position regarding women clerks with other railway companies, as well as what is happening with the GWR in the wider context.

October 7 1876

Dear Sir,

We have again very fully and carefully considered the proposal that female clerks should be employed in lieu of male clerks, in the offices and at stations.. and we have made enquiry as to the practice of the other Railway Companies. We cannot find that any of the Companies have as yet placed females in the Passenger Booking Offices, but the L & NW Co., have, to some extent, employed them at some of the principal goods stations. Neither the Great Northern or the Midland Cos., however, have yet done so.

You will observe from the reports of the District Officers, that generally speaking they do not recommend the employment of female labour, and that the whole of them, with the exception of W Bill, are indisposed to give the experiment a trial.

It is of course essential that in the case of employment of female clerks, appropriate office accommodation should be provided for them and that they should be placed under the control of a Matron, who should be responsible to the head of the office. The Superintendents and Goods Managers state that no stations on the Line have at present such accommodation as would enable the experiment to be made and that only, and until, separate office offices are provided, it is inadvisable to make a change.

Our own personal feeling is in favour of the proposal having a trial, but we are of the opinion that the experiment can be best made where there is a large establishment, such as in the Audit and Registration Offices, where a portion of the work is of a confined and regular character, or where, at any country station, the Agent or Station Master has a daughter or sister, with the necessary education and qualifications for issuing tickets and making up the accounts in the Booking Office. We have considered whether the experiment could advantageously be tried at any of the Booking Offices on the Line, such as Paddington, Reading, Leamington, Oxford, Banbury, Warwick, Wolverhampton, etc., and we are of the opinion that unless there is a complete staff of female clerks capable of doing the whole of the indoor work of a station, which we very much doubt, the proposal would be impracticable, unless the male and female clerks work together, in the same office, which is clearly objectionable.

With regard to the goods stations, notwithstanding the views of the Goods Managers, we think that female labour might advantageously be used for a portion of the work, of some of the principal stations, where there is a large number of clerks, such as Paddington, Birmingham and Bristol. At Paddington there is at present, no separate accommodation where they could work, and we do not see how it could be provided except at very great expense.

We are inclined to give the proposal a trial at Birmingham and we recommend that the experiment should be made there. At the present time the offices at Hockley are insufficient and in any case, it will be necessary to provide additional accommodation. A plan has been prepared at an estimated figure of £1,170. If the new offices are constructed and they must be, even if female clerks are not employed, we would suggest that they should be occupied by females, and it will be seen that W Bill states that he could effect a saving of about £300 in his annual expenses by the substitution of female for male labour. If the scheme works well, it can be extended to other places.

With regard to Bristol, the Goods staff are now occupying the old B & E [Bristol & Exeter] offices, where there is good accommodation, and it might be possible to employ female clerks there, but we should rather defer doing so, until we see the result of the experiment at Birmingham, more especially as the work at Bristol is now in a transition state in consequence of the amalgamation of the B & E and G W Staff.

We are, dear Sir,

Yours faithfully…

The outcome of this report is that the Board decided that a trial should be made and Minute No.1972 of the meeting of the goods managers on 24 November 1876 records:

It was considered that the experiment of employing female clerks should first be tried at Birmingham, Bristol and Plymouth, and subsequently at Paddington.

Arrangements on the following points have yet to be made:

Regulation of Employment

Scale of Salaries

Guarantee, if any.

That is it! After all that flurry of excitement, nothing seemingly happened, because a letter, dated 26 July 1905, starts the whole process of considering and enquiring all over again. They are back at square one. What happened? Samuel Cohn proposes that this new, supposedly cost-cutting exercise, brought about surprising repercussions in that managers saw an opportunity for the refurbishment and redevelopment of their offices and began 'submitting requests for remodelling of their offices using as their rationale a desire to incorporate women workers'. Cohn writes that what was to have been a cost-cutting exercise was escalating into a potentially expensive precedent-setting trend and so the whole plan was dropped. I can find nothing to support this, but it does seem a plausible theory as the whole 'woman proposal' appears to have been completely abandoned.

The next recorded documentation to be found regarding female clerks is not until 1905, some twenty-nine years later, when the matter is raised again. Representatives of GWR attending the International Railway Congress in the United States noted that 'the American Lines employed a number of lady clerks'. The United States were, at this time, considered to be leaders in progressive railway management and so the general manager, Mr James C. Ingles, wanted the matter investigated in respect of the possibilities at Paddington and 'larger centres'. Once again the same issues are raised as objections by various offices and some other interesting aspects highlighted:

Audit Office, Paddington

August 5 1905

Employment of Lady Clerks in the G W Service

… the question as to whether women and girls could be employed on the staff of the audit office has been carefully considered, and it would appear that they could only be engaged upon a section of work which is 'self-contained', as it would be very objectionable to their working in departments alongside men and lads. The only section of this kind in this office is the ticket sorting and checking department where there are at present thirty-three lads and three adult clerks.

There is no doubt that the work of this section could be carried out quite as well, and perhaps more expeditiously by girls instead of lads, but I do not think that there would be any saving in the expense of this department, whilst at the same time we would lose the valuable advantage which the ticket audit office now possesses of being a training ground for lads to qualify them for leading positions on the staff here, or for supplying clerks to fill vacancies in other departments in Paddington.

There are other disadvantages against the employment of lady clerks which may be briefly summarized thus:-

1  The cost of providing separate lavatory accommodation.
2  Greater liability to sickness than in the case of lads and men, and consequent loss of staff power.
3  Unless the women and girls are admitted to the Superannuation Fund the falling off in the number of contributors would seriously affect the stability of the fund.

Looking at the suggestion all round I am unable to recommend the employment of women and girls in the various departments of this office.

D. W. Price

Mr D. Wyatt of the registration office raises concerns regarding the unavoidable contact brought about by the nature of the work and writes: 'The men clerks could not therefore be prevented from associating with the women clerks. This is a serious objection.' The officer of the Stationery & Ticket Printing Office responded:

My experience is that for shorthand, typewriting and correspondence generally, girls are quite as reliable as men. They are also most useful at the telephone, but I do not favour the employment of girls unless arrangements can be made for them to occupy a separate office.

Another point so far as my department is concerned, the want of separate lavatory accommodation for the sexes. In the new offices, etc. now being built for me I have anticipated the possible employment of girls and have arranged for this, but as my department is now, the employment of girls cannot be entertained.

It is decided to wait for the new accommodation that is already in process and Minute No.4445 records:

It is intended to recommend that an experiment be made in the employment of female clerks at the Paddington goods station as soon as the new offices have been completed, it being practicable for the necessary accommodation to be provided by a slight modification in the plans of the building. The staff in question can, it is anticipated, be advantageously employed in the preparation of accounts, abstracting and other similar duties.

When the women are finally taken on, it is recorded in a small, nondescript, handwritten note, 'female clerks have, since the attached was written, been examined and put on in the Goods Department, Paddington'. It is dated 3 August 1906 and signed D.V. LeVian…[3]

Any young woman who fancied a clerical post with the GWR in the early 1900s had to meet certain specified criteria. She had to be aged between fifteen and twenty years (twenty-five in certain circumstances) be prepared to 'undergo an examination as to her qualifications', provide three testimonials and her birth certificate as well as a certificate signed by a 'qualified medical man' declaring her to be 'free of infirmity of body or mind and of sound constitution'. She would also have to have been single and willing to resign her appointment on the occasion of her marriage. Other criteria, unspecified but understood, included being prepared to accede to male governance, always be paid at a lower wage and expect little or no promotional prospects. In return for this the GWR female clerk would achieve a certain social status amongst her peers, enter a working regime similar to that of the school room, 'be allowed twelve working days

The First World War brought 'a brave new world' for young women clerks and tracers in the drawing office, Reading. This photograph, taken outside the building shows Elsie and Ella Winterton (first left and front row, fourth from the left) who entered in 1915 and 1916 and went on to become draughtswomen and have long careers in the railways.

annual holiday and be entitled to the same privileges as the male staff as regards to residential season tickets, privilege tickets and free tickets'.[4]

The first female clerical workers 'put on in the Goods Department, Paddington,' were later followed by telegraphers (1908) and tracers(1910) who were to do 'some of the rough work' also at Paddington station. The earliest female clerical work record I have found shows that a Miss Minnie Violet Southwell, born 19 February 1895, started as a 'clerk (2)' in Marlow House, Swindon on 28 December 1910, aged fifteen years. She was paid 8s per week. Her great-nephew Mr John Plaister's family records show that also working there at that time was Lily Plaister, John's great aunt, who was to become Minnie's sister-in-law when she married Lily's brother Jim. Minnie was also very active in the Temperance Union. The Union played a major role in railway people's lives, both in work and in the community. Its *raison d'être* was to promote abstinence from alcohol and so it created many teetotal social opportunities to distract people from the perils of drink! Much like the anti-slavery campaign, the Union gave women opportunities to go into public spaces where they would normally have no place and allowed them a measure of influence and significance. Minnie achieved notable recognition when, through her zealous endeavours, she became the first woman to gain the Union's Gold Medal for recruiting members in 1922. Minnie's work record shows that she remained in the Company's service working through the First World War and afterwards, for a total of almost twenty-five years, before leaving to get married on 27 April 1935, when she would have been forty-years old. She received the Company's £10 Marriage Allowance. She re-entered the service five years later, as Mrs Jim Plaister, in May 1940 as a 'temporary clerk (2)', the same position she had held previously, presumably recalled because of the war. She resigned with the NSO permission in June 1943 (no explanation given) and re-entered yet again in December 1943, as a part-time clerk earning 60s per week. She worked a full day on Monday and afternoons for the rest of the week and no weekends. She finally resigned on 14 February 1944 to leave, in line with Company requirements, when she was fifty. Minnie, one of the earliest female clerical recruits, certainly at Swindon, had a long, although intermittent, working connection with the GWR, spanning almost thirty-five years. She was one of the earliest women to have a clerical career with the GWR.

Although initially very small, female clerical numbers soon grew so that in 1912 the general manager decided that a 'standardisation of conditions and regulations be laid down as to their employment, scale of wages, retirement, privileges'. The female staff were to be divided into two sections: Section A consisted of clerks, typists and tracers. This grouping was to be ordinarily appointed at ages sixteen to twenty inclusive. Section B was made up of telegraph staff and Swindon statistical staff. The women were appointed at ages sixteen and seventeen inclusive.

It was required that candidates pay a fee of 5s for a medical and sit a 'qualifying educational test arranged by the general manager'. A wages scale was established differentiating not only between Section A and Section B but also between London and provincial stations and other stations.

| Section A | London & Provincial Stations | | Other Stations | |
|---|---|---|---|---|
| At age | Commencing rate per week | Maximum rate per week | Commencing rate per week | Maximum rate per week |
| 16 | 12s | | 8s | |
| 17 | 14s | | 10s | |
| 18 | 16s | 30s | 12s | 26s |
| 19 | 18s | | 14s | |
| 20 | 20s | | 16s | |
| **Section B** | | | | |
| When learning | 4s | | 4s | |
| When qualified & waiting appointment | 6s | | 6s | |
| When appointed at age 16 | 12s | | 8s | |
| 17 | 14s | 30s | 10s | 30s |

The other stations are identified as being Birmingham, Bristol, Plymouth, Cardiff, Swansea, Liverpool and Manchester.[5]

It is not long before the numbers of female clerks was dramatically increased again. Government legislation, i.e. the Railway Accounts Bill of 1911, implemented from 1 January 1913, gave them an unexpected helping hand as new posts were created to meet its heavy requirements,[6] and by 4 August 1914 the GWR employed '278 women who were engaged on clerical duties – mainly typists, shorthand writers, telegraphists and telephone operators'.[7]

The so-called 'invasion' of women into railway offices was apparent on many levels – not only were they appropriating the male clerk's job they were also appropriating their title and status. A Mr J.R. Bennet writing in the *Magazine* (December 1915) says 'the first question to be asked by the male portion of the clerical staff is how will the employment of female clerks affect us?'

The 'Ladies from Mr. Stamper's accounts', Swindon Works, June 1916. Many of these girls joined in 1912. Elsie May Calladine (second row, end right) joined on the first day of 1912 aged fifteen, as a telephone and telegraph learner, before moving on to a clerical position. Freda Dening (third right, second row) was only fourteen when she joined that year. Constance Dawson and Eve Davies joined as a clerks in July, aged sixteen and fifteen respectively. Front row, left to right (all maiden names are given): Constance Dawson; Miss Thomas; G. Noble; M. Trebilcock; M. Davies; G. Buckland. Second row, left to right: M. Wright, G. Solven, Miss Moulden, H. Dowding, Freda Denning, L. Kirby, Elsie Callandine. Third row, left to right: P. Peters, O. Gabb, N. Tomkinson, E. Swatten, G. Godsell, N. Ford, O. Fido, Eve Davies. Back row, left to right: A. Tolchard, J. Powell, E. Mockeridge, M. Carpenter, E. Field, K. Bury, H. Craddock, M. Brown.

Clerks employed at GWR goods station, Bristol. This almost looks like a school photograph, so young do many of these girls look in their regulation uniform of white blouse and long dark skirt.

The male clerks were in disarray and anxious about a new breed of office workers like this pleasing young woman. What to call them? Female clerk? Anthropoid ape? Such names were suggested on the pages of the *GWR Magazine*. This is Marion Bruton, later Cox, who joined the GWR at Swindon Works in 1914 and worked in the Locomotive Works' manager's wages office and later in the Swindon Works' ticket office situated at the tunnel entrance to the Works, dealing with staff travel arrangements. Marion left in 1929 to marry to Gladstone Cox who worked in the accounts office as auditor.

The title of clerk carried a certain prestige, not only within the railways but also in the outside world. In this battle of the sexes the men fought hard to label the women as something 'other' to themselves. Lively skirmishes were fought on the pages of the *Magazine*. For male correspondents the issues revolved around which title carried enough respect to keep the credibility of their position yet at the same time showed the woman in her rightful place, i.e. not equal to man. To the men 'female clerk' signalled the establishing of a new regime and a significant loss to them. Women clerks brought a different perspective on the matter. What they wanted was a title that would not only establish them firmly in the workplace alongside their male colleagues, but also one that gave them an aspect of independence, carried an air of modernity and imparted some sophistication and credibility. 'Woman clerk' was not helpful as it suggested 'a portly old dame' and neither was 'girl clerk' as it gave the impression of a frivolous, 'flapper type' suggested one female correspondent. A Miss E. Denison-James makes a spirited attempt to assist this identification when she identifies herself as: 'one of those new importations labelled "the female clerk".' She moves to ask the aforementioned Mr Bennet, 'has the Company perhaps found the missing link, some more advanced type of the anthropoid ape in the female clerk?'

A new female position introduced during the First World War was that of the 'messenger girl'. The first messenger girl, employed in 1915 in the office of the Superintendent of the Line, was heralded in the *Magazine* along with a small photograph. No other details are given. Indeed it is surprising that she was given such an accolade at all being of such a lowly status. It was obviously her novelty value as at that time the GWR was keen to show how it was adapting to the new world thrust upon society by the war. She was probably taken on as a temporary war recruit but she led the way for other girls in an area of employment that was to last until the end of the GWR and after.

Working as a messenger, or in modern day parlance a 'gofer' – 'go for this or go for that' was a traditional route into employment with the GWR. It was a position that grew into existence because of the need for immediate communication and response between offices and workshops, offices and stations or any inter-department communication, in the early days before telephones. Even after telephones had been installed, the job of messenger still persisted as the need for

The first messenger girl as heralded by the
*GWR Magazine* in 1915.

somebody to take a message remained. In later years once the precedent had been established, the girls, like the boys, would start straight from school, afterwards the boys would go on to apprenticeships while the girls generally went into clerical work.

Being a messenger was an exciting job for a young person fresh out of school. It came with a fair amount of responsibility, which varied according to the office one was attached to. Edith Davis applied to be a messenger girl, sometimes referred to as an office girl, at Wolverhampton in November 1917. Even at the tender age of fourteen and a half years, Edith was on her second full-time job. Her first employment was with Messrs Baker & Crockett, hardware merchants in Wolverhampton, where she had started straight from school, earning the princely sum of 7s a week. During the six months she was with them, Edith had proved 'very satisfactory'. The reason given for her leaving them was 'to join the GWR service'. From her GWR application form we know that Edith's father, Roland Davis (although typed up as Davies) worked as a clerk in the Carriage Department, Victoria Basin, which probably helped her application. She was taken on in the office of the stores department on the 26 November 1917, at 6s per week plus 3s 9d war bonus, 'in place of J. Meakin, transferred to B stores'. One year later in December 1918 Edith is again on the move, but this time still within the GWR. We know this from Amy Read's application form which states under her 'why taken on?' 'In place of E. Davis, who filled the position vacated by A.M. Carter, transferred to Special Police Department, Paddington.' Whilst Amy was still being paid the same weekly wage as Edith had been in 1917, i.e. 6s per week, the 'war wage' had by then leapt to a staggering 10s 3d. Before the war it would have been totally unbelievable that such young girls would be earning wages like that *and* in an office. By the end of the war the GWR had employed 111 females as messengers.

A messenger's job required certain qualities and aptitudes. One had to respond quickly to a summons, listen intently and follow instructions exactly. One had to have a good knowledge of the layout of the sites and local area, keep one's wits about one when collecting and delivering various items to avoid colliding with any delivery vehicles, tractors or trains and one had to make sure to deliver the message or item to the right place and person. Suitable clothing was a necessary requirement for the girls, i.e. skirts or dresses of an appropriate length to protect one's modesty when running up and down the numerous flights of stairs, as Mrs Vera Radway discovered shortly after starting as a messenger girl in the Telephone and Telegraph Exchange at Swindon in the early 1920s:

> The nurse supervisor made a complaint about the length of my skirt. I was called in very quietly and told that my skirts were too short. I was amazed. I never thought of anything like that, well I wasn't long out of school. They weren't all that short. They used to come down below my knees, but I had to have them lengthened.

The messenger job also required stamina and a good pair of shoes to cope with the considerable amount of walking that was required, not all of it on official business, as doing 'favours' for the workers, was an accepted if unofficial part of the job. Lorna Dawes recalls during her messenger days, c.1940s, being asked many times to buy lardy cakes, a local favourite in Swindon, from Gray's Cake Shop in Bridge Street, whilst out on messages in the town. Another essential requirement was to know when to have a sense of humour. There were certain 'rites of passage' that, down the decades, had been tried and tested on each intake of unsuspecting new young messengers. Several women interviewed remember being sent for 'a bucket of steam'.

Messengers' responsibilities differed according to the office they worked in. A big part of Vera Radway's job in the Swindon Exchange was to collect the payments for each employee's private telephone calls. This entailed going around the offices and presenting individuals with their charges and collecting the money for payment. This also included 'the big bosses'. Vera recalls: 'Lots of people were terrified to go in some of these bosses offices, but I had to. It was their personal business, so I could only take it from them.' Being a messenger came with a certain amount of freedom. One had plenty of scope to stop and talk and see what was going on. It was a freedom that many missed when they were eventually contained within one work place. Vera found the confines of the Telephone and Telegraph Exchange very claustrophobic after her freedom as a messenger: 'I really liked going round the offices and meeting the different people. I found it boring when I had to stay in one place with the same people all the time.'

Lorna Dawes started her working life as a GWR messenger in April 1945, just before VE Day:

> I loved my job as a Messenger. Each morning I started by sorting copies of the previous day's outgoing post. Then every morning I had to collect a bank bag from the head messenger's office and take it to the Railway Bank in London Street. I also called at the main entrance to collect the time book. This recorded the salaried staff who had left the Works the previous day. It showed the time and the reason they left, such as a dental appointment at the GWR Medical Fund Building. I had to take the book to the various office chiefs for them to give covering signatures showing that all was in order. In the afternoon I was sent here, there and everywhere maybe to get signatures on letters from the various officers, or collect supplies such as string or soap from the general stores, or sometimes act as a guide to visitors who didn't know the Works well, so that they wouldn't go astray. Sometimes I was sent to offices outside the Works such as the Enginemen and Firemen's Sick Fund. All day long I would be up and down the tunnel like a yo-yo between Works' offices, outside offices, Park House and whatever shops I went to on errands.
>
> It was part of my job to collect the tea. In those days we didn't have tea ladies and a trolley service but there were hot-water urns under the main stairs where I would queue with a large teapot. The washing up fell to me as well, usually around twenty cups. Another of my 'food' jobs was to collect

Lorna Dawes remembers that being a messenger also meant running unofficial messages, such as buying lardy cakes up the town in Swindon. Here Lorna paddles in the sea on the Isle of Man, her first office outing in 1945.

sandwiches from the underground canteen in the Locomotive Works for the office people working overtime. I remember that the sandwiches were the doorstop variety made for men on heavy jobs and I well remember a rather fragile male clerk being quite overwhelmed by their sheer size. The Loco canteen also had supplies of sweetened cocoa powder which was a real luxury as there were still shortages. The powder was put into foolscap envelopes at the canteen and was later enjoyed by me and my friends at the cinema when we dipped in wet fingers to suck whilst watching the film.

A messenger was a separate grade of work. It was not a clerical position as was clearly pointed out to Beryl Wilkins in a letter from Mr G.F. Bloxall, of Swindon Works, dated 15 December 1941. He states: 'I have vacancies for female office messengers and if you are prepared to accept such a position will you please arrange to attend this office for interview... It must be clearly understood that these are not clerical posts.'

This was in response to Beryl's letter of application where she had innocently (or cheekily) written that she was 'desirous of obtaining employment as a clerk in the service of the Great Western Railway', this at the fresh young age of fourteen and straight from school!! Beryl had provided an excellent 'certificate of character' from her school where her 'regularity' and 'diligence' were described as 'very good', whilst her 'punctuality' and 'conduct' were 'excellent'. Her headmistress had also written: 'Beryl is a very steady worker, thoroughly trustworthy and has very pleasant manners.' She commenced work as a temporary employment office messenger in the stores department on 22 December 1941.

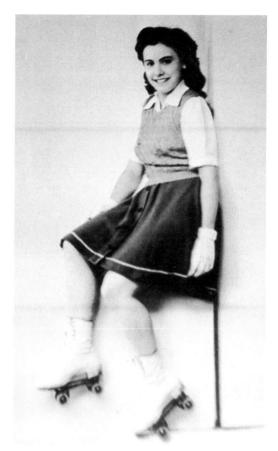

Mrs Betty Curtis, here aged fourteen, loved her job as messenger girl 'Inside' Swindon Works in the early 1940s. She also loved rollerskating which took place each week at the Milton Road Baths when the pool would be boarded over for the evening. Betty often said 'It would have been great to take my skates to work. I'd have got around a lot quicker!' Betty, who like many girls and women at that time, made most of her own clothes, found that it paid her to put large pockets in her skirts and dresses as, although things were generally scarce, as she went round the factory, the older men, retained or brought back for the war years, would give her little treats of fruits, sweets and even chocolates!

Mrs Jean Edwards (*née* Skinner) was another 'innocent just out of school' – as was her soon to be lifelong friend and eventual sister-in-law, Doris Edwards – when they joined the GWR's Parcel Accounts Office of Cardiff General station on the same day in 1943, aged fourteen as office girls. 'We were kept very busy at everyone's beck and call', says Jean. Their job was much like the messengers in Swindon offices, running errands, making tea, doing the post, finding papers, but also answering the telephone. Both Doris and Jean disliked answering the phone. The reason for this was that many companies would ring up and talk in 'shorthand' expecting to be understood. One such call Jean remembers was a man saying, 'William Morgan here, we want 250 chip of mush.' Not knowing what he meant or whether it was for real and not a joke, Jean put the phone down again. Jean and Doris felt very much 'thrown in the deep end,' and were expected to cope. Incidentally what the man wanted was 250 chips, i.e. baskets, of mush – mushrooms! It would appear that Doris and Jean were the first young girls straight from school to have been taken on as Jean remembers when she started they did not know what to pay her. 'The boss, Mr James, said: "we don't usually have young girls here. What to do?" so they had to go away and think about it.' The decision that Jean's boss arrived at was a very good one for the girls as it was decided to start them on the same level as the first entry of young boys at sixteen years, £1 3s 6d. This was most unusual. To start on a pay rate for a boy was good, but for a sixteen year old when you were just fourteen was even better, especially as women and girls were always paid less than men and boys.

There were other women and young girls amongst the thirty-plus staff already working in the accounts office when Jean and Doris arrived. Pat Eylott was just fifteen; Marjorie Follett aged sixteen; Mary Ellis aged eighteen; as well as some a little older, Misses Eve Thomas, Mary Rowlands and Dorothy Jones. There was also a Miss Sylvia Cotterral, then aged forty-one, who had joined the Company when she was sixteen just before the end of the war in 1918, and, having remained single, had stayed. One of the side effects of more women in the office was that the already 'teeny, weeny' – to use Jean's description – facilities comprising one toilet and basin and a table and chair, were even more cramped. Lack of, or inadequate, female facilities was an argument the GWR had used many times to exclude women from their workplace. The existing female facilities were probably made available during the previous war when small numbers of women were temporarily brought in. Jean and her colleagues were unhappy about the situation and 'kicked up a bit of a fuss a few times' and eventually they were given a rest room which was a lot bigger, with three toilets and three wash basins, that had a cupboard , but no windows so felt 'a bit like a dungeon'. Still, the women were pleased. It was a victory for their united, collective agitation.

Jean has dramatic memories of her wartime working especially seeing the evacuees arriving as well as seeing the many wounded soldiers arrive at the station after D-Day, but her most memorable experience occurred just a few weeks after she had started work. The station was heavily bombed and the time bombs dropped were left lying on the station platforms. Jean was alarmed and frightened. She told her boss that she did not think her father would be happy knowing that she was working around time bombs. The chief clerk, Mr Gwilym Evans phoned the Divisional Office at Queens Street station and told them what she had said. Headquarters advised that all the staff be sent home. Once she got used to the work Jean enjoyed it. Working in the Parcels' Account Office was definitely a much better option than going into service. At the end of the war several of the women were kept on even when the men came back, which Jean believes started more women thinking of working for the railways. In 1949, aged twenty, Jean left to get married to Doris' brother, who also worked for the GWR.

Whilst the First World War brought more work opportunities for female clerks it created extra problems for the GWR as in many industrial centres they experienced difficulties 'in obtaining candidates possessing the necessary qualifications for [these] positions'. The reasons given for this was that 'the scheduled rates of wages are too low in comparison with rates obtaining generally', so an increase of 2s was adopted and 'Supervisory Posts', a means for advancement, were introduced.[8] The revised pay still left the GWR female clerks feeling ill-done-by and in November 1915 they petitioned the Company to 'have the same advantages … as are enjoyed by the male staff'. The memorial signed by ninety-three women but with two names suffering a change of heart or an attack of nerves and subsequently scrubbed out, points out that 'since the War the majority of lady clerks are entirely self dependent, and therefore the increased cost of living is felt with equal proportion to the male clerks, those of whom over eighteen years of age, are in receipt of 5/- weekly bonus, whereas women receive only 3 shillings.'[9] Their petition fell on stony ground as the Company recommended no further change and rates of pay and war bonuses continued to be a contentious issue over the war period.

The GWR, like other railway companies, found its administrative workload hugely increased by the demands of the First World War and new methods were sought to cut down time-consuming actions and speed up repetitive procedures. The pressures of assessing locomotive and train mileage for government special trains, as well as accounting for works carried out on behalf of the ROD and Ministry of Munitions, pushed the railway companies into finding ways to circumvent established practices. GWR Staff Minutes record the Company's determination to implement new technology, such as the Addressograph machine, to assist this. This appears to have been successful, as in December 1915 C.W. Yates, GWR's registrar based at Paddington, declares his satisfaction with the newly installed 'addressograph' and the work of the five female clerks engaged for this, so much so that he begs to request that three of the:

> senior female members be retained on permanent appointments purely for addressograph purposes – Miss Mabel Florence Parker, as clerk-in-charge, Miss Dorothy Lilian Clark as 1st Assistant and Miss Constance Ethel Clark, who have all completed twelve months service. These female clerks have conducted the Addressograph work with ability and have given me every satisfaction in the performance of their duties.[10]

As the numbers of female clerks increased so did the variety of offices they were to be found in as demonstrated by the following table:[11]

## Summary of Classification of Women and Girl Clerks Showing Total Numbers in Each Class

| DEPARTMENTS | NUMBERS | | | | TOTALS |
|---|---|---|---|---|---|
| Class | Sp1 | 1 | 2 | Jnr | |
| General Managers | 1 | 3 | 16 | -- | 20 |
| Traffic | 2 | 11 | 586 | 26 | 625 |
| Goods | -- | 9 | 681 | 20 | 710 |
| Engineering | 1 | 2 | 25 | -- | 28 |
| Locomotive | -- | 3 | 263 | 19 | 285 |
| Accountant | -- | 1 | 74 | 5 | 80 |
| Secretaries | -- | 5 | 12 | -- | 17 |
| Surveyors & Estate | 1 | 1 | 16 | 1 | 19 |
| Electric Engineer | -- | -- | 3 | -- | 3 |
| Hotels | -- | 2 | 12 | 3 | 17 |
| Signal | -- | -- | 4 | -- | 4 |
| Marine | -- | -- | 1 | 1 | 2 |
| Stores | -- | -- | 67 | 8 | 75 |
| Stationery | -- | -- | 5 | -- | 5 |
| Special Police | -- | -- | 5 | -- | 5 |
| TOTALS | 5 | 37 | 1773 | 83 | 1898 |

By 1918 this number had increased to 2,905. A number of these were newly created positions so that at the end of the war many of the women were retained.

# MEMORANDUM OF AGREEMENT

IN REGARD TO RATES OF PAY AND CONDITIONS OF SERVICE OF
RAILWAY WOMEN AND GIRL CLERKS.

It is agreed that all Women and Girl Clerks employed by the Controlled Railways
f England, Scotland and Wales, and the Railway Clearing House, shall, for the purpose
f fixing the new rates of pay, be allocated by the employing Company or the Railway
learing House, to one or other of the undermentioned classes, and be paid on the scale
f pay applicable to the class in which they are placed.

1.—SCALES OF PAY.

The new scales of pay to come into operation as from August 1st, 1919, are
as follows :—

### GIRL CLERKS.

|  | Per week. |
|---|---|
|  | s. d. |
| At 16 years of age     ...     ...     ...     ... | 17. 6 |
| On joining at or attaining the age of 17 years     ... | 21  6 |

### WOMEN CLERKS.

#### Class 2.

Girl Clerks will pass into the Second Class at age 18, subject to good conduct,
also to successfully passing the examinations prescribed by the employing Company.

Women Clerks in the Second Class will be paid at the rate fixed for their age,
as under :—

| Age in years. | | | | | | | Per week. |
|---|---|---|---|---|---|---|---|
|  |  |  |  |  |  |  | s. d. |
| 18 | ... | ... | ... | ... | ... | ... | 30  0 |
| 19 | ... | ... | ... | ... | ... | ... | 32  0 |
| 20 | ... | ... | ... | ... | ... | ... | 34  0 |
| 21 | ... | ... | ... | ... | ... | ... | 36  0 |
| 22 | ... | ... | ... | ... | ... | ... | 38  0 |
| 23 | ... | ... | ... | ... | ... | ... | 40  0 |
| 24 | ... | ... | ... | ... | ... | ... | 42  6 |
| 25 | ... | ... | ... | ... | ... | ... | 45  0 |
| 26 | ... | ... | ... | ... | ... | ... | 47  6 |
| 27 | ... | ... | ... | ... | ... | ... | 50  0 |
| 28 | ... | ... | ... | ... | ... | ... | 52  6 |
| 29 | ... | ... | ... | ... | ... | ... | 55  0 |
| 30 | ... | ... | ... | ... | ... | ... | 57  6 |
| 31 | ... | ... | ... | ... | ... | ... | 60  0 |

#### Class 1.

|  | s. d. |
|---|---|
| Minimum     ...     ...     ...     ...     ... | 65  0 |
| After two years     ...     ...     ... | 67  6 |
| After two years (maximum) ...     ...     ... | 70  0 |

Whilst the First World War pushed up wages in general, especially with the inclusion of the war bonus, female clerks were still paid a lot less than their male colleagues. After the war, all railway wages had to be re-adjusted according to this agreement negotiated between the Ministry of Transport, the RCA and the NUR, which still incorporated the male-female differential.

An Annual Census of Staff for the Centenary year of the GWR in 1935 showed that: 'the total number of officers and clerks is 10,896, including 1,618 women and girl clerks'. By this time work on most of the mechanised office machinery was seen as 'female skills' and there were many 'female-only' offices.

The attraction and appeal of clerical work in GWR's offices had not lessened. It was regarded as 'a thoroughly good job', or 'quite something' and women were proud to be there. In Swindon there were always more applicants than posts available as highlighted by the experience of Miss Betty Whatley. In December 1937, aged sixteen, she wrote to the General Manager's Office, Swindon Works: 'I wish to make application to sit at the forthcoming examination for lady clerks to be held at Swindon.'[12] The examination was extensive covering: 'Dictation and handwriting; arithmetic; general knowledge; shorthand; typing.' An example of such an examination held at the PRO, as completed by Betty in 1938 shows that, at this time, the emphasis was placed on mathematics and spelling. Questions such as 'Reduce 6,789,012 inches to miles, furlongs, poles, etc.' and 'What is the interest upon £235 17s 6d for six years at 3½ per cent' were asked. All workings out had to be shown. There were also general knowledge questions such as:

The GWR originally operated an upper-age limit of twenty-five years for temporary staff, as stated in a letter dated January 1924 to Miss Ada Winifred Griffiths: 'You will no doubt observe that the usual maximum age of twenty-five years is one of the conditions of temporary women clerks' (unfortunately, she was thirty-six). All women, temporary or permanent, had to leave on their marriage; because of this, female staff were always thought of as temporary and so were not included in a pension fund until 1938.

# GREAT WESTERN RAILWAY

GENERAL MANAGER'S OFFICE,
PADDINGTON STATION, W.2.
*25th March, 1938*

DEAR MADAM,

### PROPOSED PENSION FUND FOR FEMALE CLERKS.

The Directors have had under consideration for some time the question of the establishment of a Pension Fund for Female Clerks, and as you are on the Register of Appointed Female Clerks I enclose for your information a copy of the Rules of a contributory scheme which will be put into operation as from the 4th April, 1938.

Broadly, the scheme provides for existing Female Clerks on the appointed staff to be admitted, irrespective of age, at the rate of contribution appropriate to the age at which they entered the Company's service. The Company will contribute to the scheme a sum sufficient to establish it on a sound financial basis, and will also contribute annually a sum equal to the contributions of the members, together with interest at 4% per annum on the moneys of the Fund. In the case of members who leave the service before completing 10 years' membership of the Fund, the Company will make arrangements for the return of those members' own contributions.

It is an essential condition of the scheme that all new entrants into the service as Female Clerks will be required to join the Fund on appointment provided they are not more than 36 years of age. In the case of new entrants over this age, admission to the Fund will be subject to special arrangements.

Pension Allowances will be based on length of continuous service with the Company and period of membership of the Pension Fund, in accordance with Rule 7, and will be granted independently of any State Pension for which a member may be eligible.

The Pension Fund will be administered by a Committee of Management, consisting of five persons representing the members and five Officers of the Company.

Examples of the operation of the Fund and of approximate weekly contributions of members are appended.

Will you kindly complete the enclosed form, indicating whether or not you desire to join the Female Clerks' Pension Fund, and return it WITHOUT DELAY to the Secretary of the Fund in the accompanying envelope? Under the provisions of Rule 2, the period within which the option to join the Pension Fund may be exercised expires on the 30th June, 1938, but as the Fund will operate as from the 4th April, an early reply will be appreciated.

Yours faithfully,

Who wrote the following:
*The Heart of Midlothian*
*The Mill on the Floss*
*A Tale of Two Cities*
*The Pilgrim's Progress*
*The Jungle Book*
*GWR FORM (3063-2A) STEAM Museum Swindon*

In what countries lived (or live):
Peter the Great
Washington
Mussolini
Robert the Bruce
Bach

In 1939 Betty, now eighteen, wrote again, this time directly to Mr J. Kelynack, in the Chief Mechanical Engineers' Department: 'I am making an informal application for a post as female clerk on the Railway Clerical Staff for which I passed the entrance examination in 1938.' Mr Kelynack's reply is short and not very reassuring: 'I will retain your name on my list in case we have a suitable vacancy to offer, but I would point out my list of passed candidates is a very long one.' It is not until November 1939 that Mr Kelynack writes to her enquiring if she is 'still desirous of being considered for employment in these offices'. She was then offered 'employment in replacement of staff serving with HM Forces, terminable by one week's notice'.

The mileage office 1923, one of the 'female-only' offices in Swindon Works. These women were comptometer operators. Their job was to cast statistical figures for month ending accounts. G.J. Churchward created the office in 1913, in the old 'D' shop, Brunel's wheel turnery, to accommodate the new increased intake of female clerical staff to deal with the requirement of new Government legislation. Front row, third left: Anessa Allen. Second Row, second left: Mrs Constance Alice Horne (*née* Griffin).

This is a fantastic photograph showing an array of office machinery that was operated by women in another female-only office. The women sitting are electro-mechanical punch operators. These cards were punched with holes, according to the criteria set, such as wages, and the women could 'read' the holes as easily as reading words. The machines on the left are tabulators and those at the far end are sorting machines. All the punched cards would be filed in the hundreds of little filing draws on the right. It is interesting to note the mirror on the wall at the end, especially as even in the Second World War, many GWR female employees' cloakrooms did not have such a luxury!

If the the First World War was the time that really allowed women *entrée* into railway offices, then the Second World War was the time when, to quote local wisdom, 'women flooded them'. This was not just the main offices, but also in stations, dockyards and goods depots, up and down the system. In early 1940 Mrs Margaret Doubleday (*née* Hill) was employed as a secretary in a patent agent's office in Birmingham. She lived in Bilston, near Wolverhampton, and bombing raids were making travelling to and from work increasingly difficult. Her father, Howard Hill, a GWR chief inspector at Birmingham Moor Street goods station, suggested she should try to get a job with the GWR nearer home. After an interview and a shorthand and typing test at Birmingham Snow Hill station, Margaret was accepted to work in the 'Correspondence' office of Herbert Street goods station, Wolverhampton. On 2 June 1940, aged twenty, she reported for duty:

> It was very different to my previous job. First, the offices, although not that old in actual age, were far from modern – almost Dickensian – so different from the modern offices in Birmingham city centre. The other difference was that from day one I was called by my Christian name, or rather I was called Peggy, as there was already another Margaret working there.

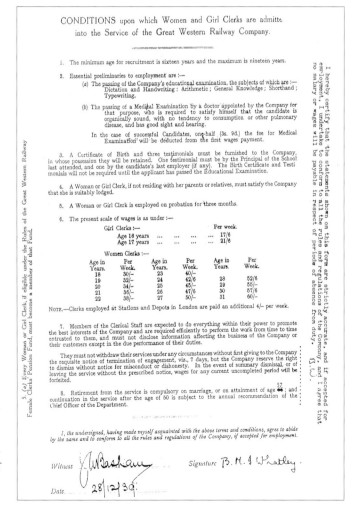

Beryl Whatley's persistence in applying to the GWR eventually paid off, although her employment was only on a temporary war basis. The age of recruitment had changed so that now the maximum was just nineteen years, presumably because of the requirements of the newly introduced pension fund in 1938.

When asked if she was surprised by this, considering the reputation of formality that railway offices had at that time, Margaret replied: 'Yes, I was surprised, but in those days railway offices were very friendly; most of us had fathers or brothers on the GWR and so our names were already known.' When asked whether the women called the men by their first names Margaret said: 'Yes, the ones we worked with, but not the management, they were all treated with great respect.'

There were a number of different offices within the goods station. Wages, cashier and accounts, all came within the correspondence office accommodation and, in separate offices in another part of the building were the delivery and invoicing departments. Margaret continues:

When I started there was one messenger boy, five men and myself. I replaced another woman typist. There were two long desks in my office with five people at each desk, but we had plenty of space. The other offices within the goods station were the same. The windows were big and gave a good light, but they were rather high up. They had very effective blackout blinds and once they were drawn we could use the electric lights normally. My typewriter was an Oliver. It was really ancient! Later I had a Royal. There were no other facilities apart from a separate toilet with a small mirror. The only comfort was your chair! Heating was not too good. It was very restricted during the war, and after for a time. Our office had radiators, but the invoicing and delivery offices, had open fires, which often smoked and filled the office with fumes from the poor quality fuel. Sometime we were so cold we had to resort to wearing our jackets, or even our coats!

Despite the cruelly cold winters that seemed to permeate the war years, the GWR were constantly urging their employees to 'exercise every care to prevent wastage or misuse of coal, gas or electricity'. This came on top of the Government's Waste of Fuel Order initiative of 1942 which prohibited 'wasteful and uneconomic use of fuel of any kinds'. One other memory Margaret has of her office, which will seem alien in these days of Health and Safety was 'the office fug':

Nearly all the men, and some of the women, smoked. The office had a permanent 'fug' of tobacco smoke in the air. There was no taboo about women smoking in the offices, despite the fact that 'outside' there was something of a feeling that women who smoked were rather risqué and although a man could walk the streets with a cigarette hanging from his mouth, a woman smoking in the street would have been frowned upon and thought of as common.

Margaret's job was to take dictation from the goods agent, Mr E. Lampitt, the senior member of staff, as well as Mr P. Chance, the chief clerk and her immediate boss, Tommy Lowe, who was in charge of 'correspondence'. Her work day started at 9 a.m. with dictation of letters from any of these gentlemen. She would then type these up until the lunch hour, often re-using the backs of old notes and letters as part of the GWR's effort to save on paper. In those days copies were made by using carbon paper over other sheets of paper. Getting hold of carbon paper was extremely difficult so what there was, was used until literally worn out. Even with good carbon the most one could achieve was three or maybe four copies. Anything requiring multiple copies (which was heartily discouraged during the war to save on paper) would have to be re-typed, over and over again. Lunch was 1 p.m. till 2.30 p.m. and, as there were no facilities, Margaret always went home, returning at 2.30 p.m. until 6.00 p.m. to deal with letters, get them signed and ready for posting

Herbert Street goods station was a bustling place. A lot of the traffic was destined for the military and was, therefore, treated as very secret. This was especially the case in the run up to D-Day when codewords were used to identify the goods in the wagons, obviously so as not to give away the fact that a stockpile of equipment was being created somewhere. This was a new thing and the staff were soon able to 'put two and two together', however everyone was severely warned not to disclose any this information to anyone, which no one did of course, but they all realised that something big was going on.

Margaret has strong memories of the activities and changes that occurred through the war in the depot and recalls that:

> Italian prisoners of war were used as manual labour on the depot. The staff were told not to fraternise but they did talk to those who had English. They were a friendly lot and used to sing a great deal! They made no effort at all to escape but seemed to be glad to be out of the front line. What I found surprising was that they were supplied with Italian-style food – even with rationing! When I started in 1940 there were very few women working in the goods yard, as these jobs were considered unsuitable for women, but eventually, as war went on, more were recruited. Some of the women had very unsociable hours, starting as early as 6 a.m. in the delivery office or not ending until 7 p.m. or 8 p.m. in the invoicing office. Sometimes they had to work on Sundays. The delivery staff had to draw up delivery sheets for the 'Carmen' (these were the delivery drivers who for the most part had horse-drawn carts), and the invoicing staff had to prepare the invoicing documentation for forwarded traffic.

Margaret really enjoyed her job and was pleased she did not have to leave at the end of the war as she had not replaced a man – her work having previously been done by a woman, however, on the occasion of her marriage, she had to leave:

> I left the railway in 1948, after eight very happy years. I suppose in today's world I would have stayed, but when I got married most married women gave up their jobs to start running a home (there were so few labour-saving devices that running a home was pretty much a full-time job) so I just took it as normal. Whilst I was happy to become a 'housewife' it wasn't entirely my choice as there was a policy not to employ married women, which was very vigorously enforced. As soon as you knew the date for your wedding you had to inform your boss and your leaving date was scheduled as the day before. They took back your free pass travel from the day of the marriage.

By the time of the Second World War attitudes in general towards female clerks had changed. Most, if not all, of the old vast ledgers of bookkeeping had disappeared in favour of the loose-leaf file and so the inability to lift large, heavy volumes was no longer an issue regarding women's suitability for the job. Because of the experiences and precedents set in the First World War, female booking clerks, ticket clerks and information clerks up and down the line quickly lost their novelty and were accepted as normal. During the war women were generally submitted against Works order numbers from the Labour Exchange but even then one still had to have 'something about you', to obtain work in the GWR offices.

Once in the offices, all the women remembered being treated 'like ladies' by the men. During the Second World War many of these men would have been in the older age group not to have been conscripted or even returned retirees. 'They were very old-fashioned towards us, rather distant and superior but always very gentlemanly', says Mrs P.F. who took up employment as a young girl in 1940. This alongside the conservative and school-like nature of railway offices gave them a particularly old-fashioned cultural ethos which most of the women appeared to like. After the war many of the women stayed on. Attitudes had subtly changed and staff shortages still persisted. By 1947 there were 3,683 women and 445 girls making a total of 4,128 GWR female clerks.

# GREAT WESTERN RAILWAY.

## Application for Employment in Replacement of Staff Serving with H.M. Forces.

(TERMINABLE BY ONE WEEK'S NOTICE).

(38 G)

| | |
|---|---|
| Name in full. *(Surname first in block letters)* | WHELAN, HILDA MAY. |
| Address ... ... ... ... ... | 49 CLIFTON STREET, SWINDON. |
| Date and place of birth ... ... ... | 3RD MAY 1906 LONDON |
| Schools at which educated ... ... .. | CATFORD CENTRAL SCHOOL & PITMANS COLLEGE. |
| Date of leaving school ... ... ... | 1923 |
| Particulars of any educational certificates held | — |
| Present employment (if any) ... .. | — |
| Previous employment (if any) ... ... | ADMIRALTY, ROYAL NORTHERN HOSPITAL, LONDON. HOME GUARD, BESWICK & SON, SWINDON. |
| Occupation and address of father. *(If deceased, state occupation when living)* ... | DECEASED. CIVIL SERVANT. |
| Has applicant a knowledge of shorthand ? *(If so, state speed and give particulars of certificates held)* ... ... ... ... | YES. 120: R3A. CERTIFICATE |
| Has applicant a knowledge of typewriting ? *(If so, state speed and give particulars of certificates held)* ... ... ... ... | YES. 40. |
| Would applicant be prepared to accept employment at a place which would necessitate living away from home ? ... | NO. |
| Would applicant be prepared to accept temporary employment ? ... ... .. | YES. |
| When could applicant commence duty, if approved for employment ? ... ... | 15/11/43. |

| FOR OFFICE USE. | |
|---|---|
| Reference No.............. Date.................... | |

1 000·4,43·(17)—P.O.

[P.T.O.

1   PRO RAIL258/405 25140.
2   Ibid.
3   Ibid.
4   Ibid.
5   Staff Committee Minute 356, Secretary's Office, GWR Trust.
6   Alan Peck, p.184.
7   Edwin A. Pratt, p.47.
8   PRO RAIL258/405 25140.
9   Ibid.
10  Ibid.
11  Ibid.
12  CME Works Circulars and Letters, 1939–44, and Staff Records, STEAM Museum.

15 September 1939, signal engineer's drawing office, Reading. Ella Winterton (left) and colleague look up from their work as draughtswomen to be captured by the camera. The plain, workman-like, heavy cotton overalls of 1914–20s have been replaced by lighter, flower-pattern, more 'feminine' ones.

April 1940 and the signal's engineer's drawing office, Reading, has moved to Aldermaston for the war period. The GWR's employees had to find accommodation in the nearby villages in order to be able to get to work during the week. It is interesting that whilst it was still thought necessary to protect the women's clothing, this did not apply to the men, they just took off their jackets.

*Opposite:* The application forms for female staff underwent many changes over the years. This one, for clerical workers, is very specific in its intentions. Overleaf it states: 'The Company is unable to give any undertaking as to permanent employment but it is hoped that it will be possible at a later date to proceed with the appointment in the service of a proportion of the new entrants accepted for wartime employment', but this is crossed out.

# CHAPTER 5

# WARTIME WORKSHOPS

The GWR found the issue of women in the workshops doing 'men's work' just as difficult and as troublesome as they had found women in the offices, this despite the fact that they had previously created a workshop for women, who were still there. In respect of women in the offices the debate had always been discussed in terms of frailness, impropriety, and costs. In the workshops the considerations were slowing up production, upsetting the men and unions, and costs, i.e. affecting the men's take-home pay.

Whilst there is a great deal of evidence in the form of official records and photographs, to show that women were employed in workshops on other railways during the First World War, there is little paper evidence for the GWR. E.T. MacDermot, who was commissioned by Sir James Milne – when he was general manager – to write an official history of the Company, states in his book that women were taken on 'to dilute skilled labour in Swindon Works'. His words are cited in one of Frank Potter's wartime reports to the GWR Board – Potter was general manager of Swindon Works at that time. Alan Peck, however, robustly contradicts this in his work stating: 'it was suggested in 1917 that female workers should appear in the factory but Collett managed to fend off this proposal'. The reason C.B. Collett, at this time Locomotive Works' manager, gave for not taking on the women in the workshops was the same one previously used to keep them out of the offices, i.e. that the facilities (toilets and rest rooms) and conditions would not allow for it. An official drawing identified as 'lavatory accommodation for women Loco Works Swindon' dated October 1916 and written up as 'adopted', shows that toilet and canteen accommodation was instigated for female employees in the old 'K' shop, which was the coppersmith's shop. Details on the plan shows that production equipment had to be removed for this purpose. It is also known that female toilet accommodation was actually built at this site. Presumably, if there had been no female employees, the GWR would not have invested the time or money into such an initiative. In his report of November 1916 Frank Potter wrote:

> It is proposed to extend the employment of women in wages grades … and to dilute skilled labour in Swindon Works. These steps are to an extent being opposed by the men, and in the case of the mechanics it has been found necessary to arrange a meeting with the Trade Union representatives in order to come to an understanding on the subject.

There is no further mention of women dilutees in any of his other reports, but his words are corroborated by the family history of Mr David Hyde. It records that his grandmother, Mrs Fanny Hyde, and his aunt, Miss Winnie Hyde, both worked in Swindon Works during the First World War. The two women had been in domestic service in London, Fanny as a housekeeper and Winnie, her daughter, as a lady's maid. Like thousands of others in domestic service, especially after universal conscription was introduced in 1916, they left their positions and returned home to Grafton under pressure to do their bit for the war and were taken on at the Works. They then had to move into accommodation at 53 Newhall Street, Swindon, so that they could get to the Works more easily as the hours were long. They stayed in Newhall Street until the end of the war. The work they did was munitions. The GWR had a number of contracts with the Ministry of Munitions and there is photographic evidence of such work at Swindon Works.

What a shock it must have been for these two women, especially for Fanny who had been in service, all her adult life, to come from grand and comfortable houses to the filthy factory environment. Without doubt the Works was a primitive, harsh and squalid place. Alfred Williams described it as 'dingy, dirty and drab' as well as 'dark, sombre and repellent'. He says there was 'gross impurity of air' and 'bad atmospheric conditions'. He tells that as soon as you 'enter into the smoke and fume you are sure to begin sniffing and sneezing. The black dust and filth is being breathed into the chest and lungs every moment.' Undoubtedly conditions were extreme. The toilet facilities for the men were extremely basic. The workshops miserably cold or extremely hot. Sometimes the heat was such that the workmen 'remove[d] their shirts altogether'. To have women working in such situations and alongside unclothed men would, understandably, have normally been totally unacceptable to the

There were no facilities to accommodate the women coming into Swindon workshops during the First World War to work on munitions and so arrangements had to be made. These toilets and canteen were quickly erected and adapted in what was 'K' shop and is now part of the Swindon Designer Outlet Centre. The number of toilet cubicles suggest that a significant number of women had been taken on. An interesting observation made by Mr John Walter, who had worked in the Swindon drawing office and has since created a database of hundreds of different drawings and plans, is that for females in workshops there was 'lavatory accommodation for women' whilst for female clerical workers there were 'ladies toilets' identified such plans and drawings.

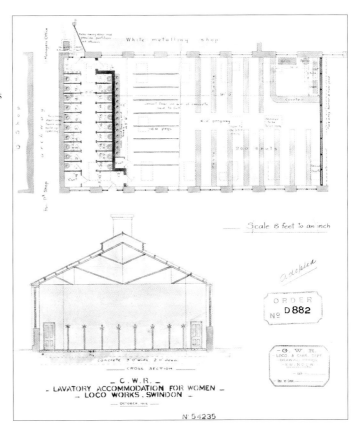

GWR, to the men, and to the local community, but the times were not normal and the country was in dire need of women workers. The women would have, as far as possible, been kept apart from the men, hence the separate canteen. It is possible, and probable, that Peck was referring to women doing 'railway work proper' in the workshops. Two decades later in the 1940s, the women recruited to the factory during the Second World War found that conditions were still very much the same. Mrs Phyllis Saunders who worked in the blacksmith's shop remembers:

It was a terrible place to have to work. It was very dirty ... dirty floors, dirty walls. It was filthy. There was not much air. There was a few windows at the top, almost up at the roof. They were seldom opened because they were a job to get to, but we did open them at times because the walls and everything got so filthy. It got hot in there. It was hot with all those open fires. I picked up a bad throat, just off diphtheria. I think it was all the dirt probably. I had some time off and the doctor treated it with Penicillin - that was twice!

Mrs Enid Saunders passionately recalls:

It was a most horrible place for a girl to work. We had no cloakroom, no locker, nothing. One of the men used to bring an old tin can with a wire handle full of hot water and put it down for us to wash our hands and we used to take our own towel. We used to hang it on a nail stuck in the wall. We had a plank of wood on two tins to sit on and there was rats running up and down the tubes.

The coppersmith's shop, Swindon Works. Three women work at repairing guards' hand lamps during the Second World War. The working conditions are pretty grim. The women are wearing their specially allocated 'free' caps, which the GWR produced in three different colours. They also wear a heavy apron on top of overalls.

The women who were already working in the Carriage & Wagon's trimming shop were altogether separate, having had the shop set up with facilities for them, and it was probably the cleanest place in the Swindon Works at that time. Williams tells us that the 'upholsterers are a class in themselves … great care and cleanliness are required for their work, they are expected to be spruce and clean in their dress and appearance.' No doubt such standards would also have been required of the women. Women working as polishers, however, would have been in a different situation, as their work was messy and dirty, as described by Mrs Kathy Grayhurst.

When it came to the Second World War Collett, now CME, had to take a different stance, yet despite writing in March 1941:

> The present and prospective situations in the matter of man power are such that it is essential from a railway point of view, as well as in the National Interest, to employ women and girls to the utmost possible extent not only in Railway Offices and Workshops but also in the Railway Operating Grades.

The intake of women was extremely slow and low. In July 1941 Collett retired and his post was inherited by F.W. Hawkesworth, who acknowledged that compared with other railway companies 'we fall far short in our efforts' regarding women employees. Unlike his predecessor he was determined not to let lack of facilities restrict the employment of women and issued notice that:

From December 1942, women between the ages of twenty and thirty (this was later extended to forty) were conscripted to war work.

**MINISTRY OF LABOUR AND NATIONAL SERVICE**

Emergency Powers (Defence) Acts, 1939-1941

DIRECTION ISSUED UNDER REGULATION 58A OF THE DEFENCE (GENERAL) REGULATIONS, 1939.

NOTE.—Any person failing to comply with a direction under Regulation 58A of the Defence (General) Regulations, 1939, is liable on summary conviction to imprisonment for a term not exceeding three months, or to a fine not exceeding £100 or to both such imprisonment and such fine. Any person failing to comply after such a conviction is liable on a further conviction to a fine not exceeding five pounds for every day on which the failure continues.

To _Miss EE Swain,_ _Employed: Exclay_
_72 Stalian Rd,_ _Swindon._
_Lower Stratton_ (Date) _30 6 44_
_Swindon_

In pursuance of Regulation 58A of the Defence (General) Regulations, 1939, I, the undersigned, a National Service Officer within the meaning of the said Regulations, do hereby direct you to perform the services specified by the Schedule hereto (see overleaf) being services which, in my opinion, you are capable of performing.

If you become subject to the provisions of an Essential Work Order in the employment specified in the Schedule, the direction will cease to have effect and your right to leave the employment will be determined under that Order. *Otherwise, this direction continues in force until* _16 1 45_ *or until withdrawn by a National Service Officer.*

I hereby withdraw all directions previously issued to you under Regulation 58A of the said Regulations and still in force.

_H. Q. Kell_

National Service Officer.

E.D. 383A.

[P.T.O.

(6/43) M38178 300M 8/43 CN&Co 748 (516)

On no account must the lack of specific accommodation – rest rooms, lavatories etc. – be allowed to hold up the employment of women in running sheds or carriage cleaning. If necessary, temporary arrangements in this connection must be made, pending the provision of permanent quarters.

Women taken on in the workshops at Swindon Works during the Second World War received a mixed reception from the men which ranged from open hostility, resigned acceptance or friendly helpfulness. 'It didn't matter what we thought, it was the war and we had to make the best of it.' This attitude as expressed by Mr X, who worked on the steamhammers, probably summarises both officials' and men's feelings regarding the matter. In the main when the women spoke about the men they worked with they would say that the men were 'gentlemen', or 'they treated us with respect'. It was only after they had been talking for a while that some would add qualifying remarks such as: 'They were nice, really, but you knew you had to get on with them', and 'There was a lot of leg pulling. It was all in fun, really.' The repeating 'really' perhaps being the most telling word underscoring as it does the women's equivocal attitude towards this 'joking'. One of the men's favourite 'jokes' was to bang the pipes near the women's workplace and make the rats scurry out. The rats were big and there were lots of them, despite the number of cats kept in the shops. The women would jump and shriek with surprise and fright. 'They thought they were so funny. They knew we hated it, hated the rats, but they would do it … again and again.' This experience was feelingly spoken of by many women interviewed and also laughingly remembered by several men. One lady remembers having her own 'special' mouse, – 'it was dead, luckily' – having been placed under her chair to startle her when she started her morning shift. 'This was a real surprise as usually it was eggshells on my chair – they used to call me "Eggo" see, because it sounded like my name.' Practical jokes were a long tradition in the workshops. Men would play them on each other, to get one over on the foreman, but especially on the apprentices and young boys. It was part and parcel of being a railwayman. With regards to the women, however, the 'playing' appeared all one way, the men on the women. Most of the women did not feel comfortable or equal enough to 'play' back, although others, like Mrs Vi Joynes, took it in their stride. After having all her teeth taken out, Vi had to wait several weeks for a set of false ones. The men took to calling her 'Gummy' and bought her a baby's bottle and dummy. At break times Vi filled the bottle with her tea and drank from it. The men thought this was a hoot and told her she was 'a good'un'. 'You had to join in,' she said. 'They could have made your life very difficult.' Phyllis Saunders found the men in the blacksmith shop were:

… quite polite, really. We soon got used to each other. They sort of treated us like boys, but still remembered that we were girls. Nobody tried anything funny. Nobody played around or did anything stupid because it was too dangerous. You had to watch things or you could get knocked with the big hammer. Us girls stuck together and we got on well with the young lads. We used to go out in a big group, just friends like.

Over time an uneasy truce operated. The men got used to having women around and many openly admitted that most women were good at their work and to work with. John Fleetwood remembers:

… in the brass foundry we had two women on the grindstones who were very good at their work, and when it came to lunch breaks they had their lunch at the bench with the men. We all got on well together. They were not frightened to get their hands dirty and they would put a deaf ear to the strong language when a chap hurt himself.

Mrs Ivy Wilson worked on munitions such as these in Swindon workshops during the Second World War. (Photograph courtesy of STEAM Museum of the Great Western Railway)

Another woman who got on well with her male colleagues, despite being accused of 'prolonging the war' by one, was Mrs Ivy Wilson (*née* Edmonds). Ivy was a fitter's mate and worked on munitions. When Ivy's husband was home on leave she would apply for permission for time off. GWR policy on this was that the married women should be 'given reasonable leave of absence', … but that they 'should utilise their annual leave … otherwise special leave granted without pay'. This was later changed so that the women did not have to use their annual leave, however, sometimes leave would still be refused. Once, when Cliff, her husband, was based at Chiseldon before moving into the field of operations, Ivy applied for a seven-day pass, which was refused. Nevertheless she stayed home with her husband for two days, then went back to work knowing she would be given a three-day suspension without pay, so she was able to spend the rest of the time with her husband after all. She used this ruse a couple of times and it was then she was accused by the foreman of 'prolonging the war'. Ivy's response was that she would see her husband whenever she could because she did not know when she would see him again. It was just as well she did, for Cliff was killed in action. 'She always gave as good as she got,' says her son Clive, 'but she always said the men were marvellous and kindly to her, especially when father was killed at Arnhem.'

Whilst working relationships may have improved, there was always an ongoing uneasiness about women doing 'men's jobs' and the GWR addressed the issue in article entitled 'Women Locomotive Builders at Swindon Works' during 1942. The article asks: 'do the women like the work?' The answer to that is obviously yes and no. Yes, some women did like the work and no, some did not, and equally some women liked some of the jobs but not all of them. Mrs E.P. recalls that during her time at the Works she was moved from shop to shop doing different jobs. She started off in the Scraggery attached to 'R' shop, nut-scragging, which she really did not like. 'It was very dirty, not a girl's job really', she says. The nuts for 'scragging' were at this stage, black,

This is Peggy who worked with Joan and Sylvia alongside apprentice Ken Gibbs operating a nut-scragging machine in the Scraggery, *c*.1946 . Nuts for facing are in the top tray, finished nuts in underneath box. Left hand wheel to 'face' the nuts, right hand small lever to taper the thread. Note Joan's apron – the nut sack!

unpolished and had had a thread put through the middle. They were left with a slightly rounded top and a very rough bottom. Nut-scragging was the process of 'facing' and 'chamfering' the nuts, that is, taking the roughness off the top and bottom and giving it a smooth 'face', and also putting a little 'chamfer' – a little, smooth slope on the inside of the nut – leading into the thread, which then assisted the threading of the nut onto the bolt. The nuts came in various sizes from quite small to the drag-hook nut which was the biggest. Working the bigger ones onto the machine was not too bad as one could find a smooth area to hold, but working with the smaller ones invariably ripped the fingers as the rough edges were very sharp. On top of that, the shop, like all machine shops, had a distinctive, heavy smell of oils, one overlapping the other, as different oils were used for tapping and facing the nuts. It could be quite nauseating. This was obviously not a fun job. It was usually a new entrant boy's job before he started on his apprenticeship. A rite of passage into factory work. It was not a job they stayed on long as Ken Gibbs, an apprentice at that time remembers. There were three women on nut-scragging when Ken was there. He remembers how they would look for small 'distractions'. One woman, Joan, was courting an electrician in the Works, and when they could escape the beady eye of Harry, the charge-hand – a rather stern character – they would make time for little chats and flirtations. Mrs E.P. wanted to escape 'scragging' so when her father, who worked in the fitting shop, heard there was a vacancy there, she quickly requested a transfer and got it. Here she did a fairly long stint on a drilling gang. After this she was moved onto bombshell turning which she 'didn't mind' but the job she really loved and so could definitely answer 'yes, she liked the work', was that of 'rivet-hotter'. This job entailed working with a mate; a 'holder-upper'. Hers was 'an older man' and she was his first female 'mate'. Once the foreman had given out the instructions for the day, the rivet-hotters, then mostly girls, were sent to collect and sort the rivets that would be needed for the job in hand. These had to be heated to red hot, then picked up by tongs and thrown to the holder-upper who would catch them in a little metal cup attached to a special glove. 'It was a hard job,' says Mrs E.P., 'especially in the summer 'cos it got so hot. We wore overalls and a heavy leather apron for protection. You just had to keep going, keeping your fire up or keeping your rivets at red hot … but not burnt because then they couldn't be used and became scrap. You had to get hold of them with the tongs and throw them across. It was hot work.' I'm not sure one could describe this as more of 'a girl's job'. It was obviously no picnic either, so it shows that Mrs E.P. was not afraid of getting hot and dirty. Perhaps it was just a matter of preference. Women also worked as holder-uppers, placing the freshly caught red-hot rivet upon the metal plate. Once placed it had to be held in position with a special large hammer and, using the handle of the hammer as a lever to push the head of the hammer against the head of the rivet whilst it was riveted, flattened in. When one realises that there would be literally hundreds of rivets in a smoke box then one also realises this was a demanding job that required sustained effort and good teamwork, so despite the men's misgivings about working with them, the women proved that they could be good 'mates'!

One woman who would have answered 'no, definitely not!' to the question raised, was Mrs Enid Saunders (*née* Swain). Enid said: 'I couldn't bear it. It was a most horrible place for a girl to

A posed photo showing a red-hot rivet about to be inserted and secured by the hydraulic riveting machine. No 'holder-up' or hammering required as the machine did it all by water pressure.

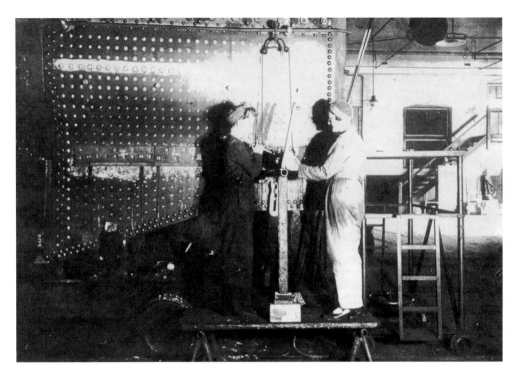

How many rivets can you count? (Photograph courtesy of STEAM Museum of the Great Western Railway)

work. Girls should never have gone in there. I did hate it.' Enid worked in the Tube House. When Enid reached twenty she was conscripted to go on war work. At the Labour Exchange she was asked if she would like to go to college and learn a trade. She studied there for three months and became a fitter. She was then sent to work at Shorts which she loved: 'It was real nice. We were all girls from all over the country. Then it closed down and I got sent to Swindon Works. When I was at Shorts I was a fitter. When I was at Swindon Works I was a dirty nobody.'

The tube shop was a small place made of corrugated iron. There were usually six girls working there. They always worked in pairs. They worked two weeks on days and then two weeks on nights doing twelve-hour shifts, 7 a.m.–7 p.m. Their job was to cut to size the tubes required to go inside the barrel of the boilers. Between them they were supposed to cut two boilers a day. Some boilers took 325 tubes. It was heavy, dirty, hard and tedious work. Enid explained:

He [the charge-hand] would give you a list of how many of each kind of tubes you had to cut. You'd go down the gangway to get them out of the rack or trucks. You couldn't lift them on your own so we used to go in twos to carry them. We had to put them on a truck and then put them on the handrack and then push them into our machine. The charge-hand used to measure them and set the machine then we had to cut them and grind them. We used to stand on a pedal and hold it down with a big handle and he [it] used to keep whizzing round and round, or jumping up and down like a jack-in-the-box, every time you cut. Then we had a truck to put them back on.

There was two of us on the cutting and grinding machine, that was Mavis and me. There were two girls on what they called 'the dirties', cutting dirty old ones. When you were on this regime, shaking all the dust sheets you used to get filthy dirty. There was two on the expanding.

Then there were four men who did the super heaters – the really big tubes. We couldn't possibly lift them.

What Enid hated most about it was that it was all so dirty: the place, the work and, because of the work and lack of facilities, herself. Enid had to wear trousers. She wore an overall coat over them and on top of that she wore the sack apron she was supplied with. On her hands she wore the big leather gloves essential for gripping the metal tubes. She did not feel comfortable or clean like this. When the girls needed the toilet they had to go through the 'L2' shop, over the traversing table and into the boiler shop, then up some stairs. They used to go in twos and were always escorted by the charge-hand, whether to be monitored or for their protection, Enid was not sure. She remembers:

> We were always so embarrassed passing all the different men. Sometimes they used to shout out to us, but they were nice, really, and he [the charge-hand] used to march behind us like a sergeant major looking at his watch. He used to stand at the bottom of the stairs and watch us go up. He used to stay there until we walked down the stairs and then march us back. He was dreadful. He was so dreadful to us that one of the girls asked for an appointment with the foreman. She told him 'I'm not going to work under him no more. You can put me where you like. You can take me to court, but I will not work under him no more.'

During the war no one could leave their war-work when they liked. Official written permission had to be applied for and given so the threat of being taken to court was real!

One area where one would not, perhaps, expect to find women enjoying the work was in the hot shops, such as the blacksmith's shop. One of the more 'colourful' images that emerged from the wartime workshops was that of the female 'hammerman'. Being a hammerman and working in a hot shop was one of those jobs that separated the men from the boys yet, during the Second World War, it became a common sight to see young, slimly built women and girls working and cleaning these impressive machines. These were machines that had, at other times, been held to be beyond women's physical capability and far too dangerous to work at. To the men who worked alongside these new recruits it must have seemed a contradiction of all the values on which their work and identities had been defined. Mrs Phyllis Saunders, then Phyllis Bezer, was twenty-years old and working at sewing in Nicholson's Raincoat Factory when she was conscripted into Swindon Works. Talking about her experiences she says:

> I was conscripted from Nicholsons, there was a lot of girls conscripted from there, and I was chosen to go into the Great Western with several other girls. We went into this great, huge place and we wandered whatever was going to happen to us. We were told we were going to do 'essential jobs'. I went to F1 blacksmith's shop. I worked with Mr Davis and there were two strikers who worked with him as well, and one hammerman, although it was hammergirl with us. I worked on a 20cwt hammer, the largest in the shop. There were several hammers all round the workshop, but they were smaller. My one was the heaviest and the biggest.

Phyllis worked in a gang of four. Apart from driving the hammer, her job was to oil the machine each morning and keep it clean, with water and wire wool, through the day. She recalled:

> It was very tiring on your arms at first. It was a different way of using your arms, not like sewing, but I got used to it and the aches and pains soon wore off. When I first got there I got ever such bad feet. I used to wear thick socks and thick shoes. We had to wear stout shoes. For the very first pair when I went in, I used my Dad's, he took a size five and so did I – I think we

Outside the Tube House of corrugated iron, Swindon Works. Middle row, left to right: -?-, Enid Saunders; Eva Dunn; Eileen 'Bubbles' Breadmore and in the middle of the front row, Amy Webb. Enid Saunders always said that the men were 'real gentlemen' and looked after the girls.

Mrs Enid Saunders hated working in the Tube House during the Second World War. 'It was a horrible, dirty place,' she said. 'You never felt clean.' Looking at how grubby (although cheerful) they all look one can understand why she felt as she did. Left to right: Jack, Enid, Eva Dunn, Len Webb, -?-, -?-, -?-.

were short of coupons just then, so I had to make do. I got really bad feet – blisters and things. I went to the chemist to see if he could help me and he told me to use surgical spirit to harden my feet up. It dried it all up and I was all right after that.

One of the women who replied, 'yes I loved the work, loved the place and loved the whole experience' was Mrs Violet Irene May Joynes (*née* Pickett), always known as Vi. She was extremely proud of her time working 'Inside' during the Second World War. 'It was,' she said on many occasions, 'the best time of my life.'

Vi's father, Joseph Pickett, a tradesman in the Works, treated Vi like a son and taught her all he knew about tools and how to use them. Vi was able to turn her hand to mending electrical appliances, re-cording sash windows or re-wiring a house, so when Vi went into 'the factory' she had no trouble learning how to use the machinery. She worked in several different shops and did many different jobs, acetylene welding, milling, grinding, turning and setting machines but it was working as an overhead crane driver that gave her, her greatest joy.

The GWR talking about the introduction of women as overhead crane drivers called it 'a daring experiment'. To see these huge pieces of mechanism moving up and down the shops does not give one the impression that it is a woman's job to drive them, they wrote and called these women 'pioneers'.

Vi Joynes was one of these 'pioneers'; in fact, she believed she may have been the first: 'I was the first woman crane driver, well female 'cos I was only a girl.' In fact, it turned out that she was too much of a girl, not legally old enough to be paid the full wage for this job so the union insisted she was 'cheap labour' and must be taken off.

Mrs Phyllis Saunders (*née* Bezer), seen on the right-hand side of the picture a new breed of 'hammerman', left her job of sewing in the raincoat factory to become a hammerman in one of the hot shops of Swindon Works when she was conscripted in 1942. This beast, 20cwt, was the biggest hammer in the blacksmith's shop. 'The Blacksmith said what blow to strike – a big heavy one or lots of little ones – and I did it,' she said.

Vi Joynes was one of the few women who talked of how the unions impacted on her time 'Inside'. She was not much taken with them as on both occasions they intervened she felt that she had lost out. The first time, as mentioned, was when the union insisted Vi be taken off the overhead cranes. Vi was bitterly disappointed but she did admit that the union was trying to protect her and others. The other time was when she was working on the turning machine. These machines required very precise calibrating. The women were not considered to be skilled enough to do this or to be trained to do it, in spite of the fact that women's contribution during the First World War had shattered the mythology that women were incapable of skilled work. The acquisition of skills was an area historically steeped in competition and bad blood, between men and men, union and union, and men, union and employer, and, undoubtedly, men and women. Skill was highly regulated and stringently controlled. In the railways it was also jealously guarded. The men were reluctant or actively against assisting the women. One woman interviewed remembers that when she and the only other woman working in the —Shop first started their job, they would find parts of their turning machine missing or loose each time they started their shift; this being the handiwork of the men using the machines on the previous shift. This became so annoying and time consuming, and, at times, even dangerous, they eventually complained angrily to the foreman, threatening to walk out if he did not sort it out. These expressions of resistance were so common that the 'shop stewards' National Council deemed it necessary to issue a stern reprimand to 'fellow workers' in October 1941.[1] The restriction of the setting of the machine by a man was part of the union's wartime re-classification of jobs strategy, whereby skilled jobs were broken down into separate parts, and the lesser or unskilled part given to women to do, thereby often classifying them as 'unskilled' labour and thus determining their level of wages. All this meant nothing to Vi. Her complaint was that she hated wasting time waiting around for the man to come to set her machine. 'I can do that,' she said and got on with setting her own and other women's machines, but that was not allowed. 'The Union man came up and said "Do you belong to the Setters' Union?" "No," I said and he said "Will you join?" and I said "I suppose I'll have to." They gave me a shilling extra on my basic pay for setting machines, and it cost me a shilling a week to be in the union, so that was that!' Other women interviewed who had worked on such machines told of how they too would get exasperated by having to wait for the 'gaffer' to calibrate their machine and so got on with it themselves, but were not paid anymore for it. When asked whether they thought this was a fair practice, the women appeared not to have worried about it. They just shrugged and said: 'That's how it was' or 'We were getting good wages compared to what we got working in Woolies' or 'Well, it was the war and we just had to get on with it.' This last response was used as the answer to many different difficulties. Later, when Vi went into the boiler shop, she had to join the NUR: 'You knew before you went in there you had to join the Union – it was a closed shop so everybody was in the Union. I had to join the NUR.' It is more than a little ironical that the NUR, the union that had fought so hard to keep women out, now insisted that they came in!

Training was a large part of skill acquisition and railwaymen spent long years being 'trained', yet during the war it was greatly reduced or forgotten about. Almost overnight one of the basic tenets of becoming a railwayman had become downgraded. When asked what sort of training she was given to go on the cranes, Vi replied:

Not much. I went up with the groundsman in the morning. He took me down the bay, taught me the hand signals, done a few lifts, then he took me back, we went down for a break and he never came back. I was left there doing what I could, so I really didn't have a lot of training, but one thing he did teach me was how to swing round girders. To get to the cranes we had to walk along the girders, horizontal ones. There was no handrail mind. Fifteen feet in the air and no handrail. There were other girders to keep the ceiling from the floor [uprights] and you had to swing round those, you had to really swing round to get to the other side, to the crane box.

Vi's experience regarding training was similar to many other women. Phyllis Saunders, when asked how she had coped with the training, remarked:

> We didn't really do anything very much. I had to go straight on the big hammer. We just had to practice on those rubber mats, one big blow or lots of up and downs. He [the Blacksmith] told me and I did it. I don't remember spending long on learning. We had to get on with it because of the war.

Later Vi had another chance to drive the cranes when she was put in the boiler shop. Although she had previous crane-driving experience she had not worked the bigger cranes necessary for lifting and turning the boilers. Her first effort was very hit and miss, in fact, as she said, 'it was very hit and hit!' as she knocked three boilers over as the lifted boiler swung round. When asked how the men responded to this she laughed. 'The men run that time, which I didn't blame them, but after that they just used to stand there and carry on with their job.' Some of the men interviewed from Swindon admitted that they had been very sceptical with regard to women overhead crane drivers but said that later they had found the women to be better than the men, because 'women had a special light touch… they could put them down on a sixpence'. When Vi first went on night shift she was told by the foreman to wear trousers. This did not sit well with her father, so when she went back on days his immediate response was 'back to frocks then girl!' Vi's job entailed climbing a ladder and walking along girders over the heads of the men below. Why it was acceptable to do this in a frock during day shift but not acceptable to do it during night shift was not clear even to Vi, but what was clear was her father's relief to get her back into frocks!

One of the reasons given for men's reluctance to welcome women on the shop floor was that they believed the women would not meet the targets and adversely affect their take home pay. Mrs Alice Coale remembers being harassed by the charge-hand to keep her up to quota for this reason:

> I went into 'AM' shop. First I was with another girl, doing war work, but then she was moved and I was on a bench with just men. Five men and me. I used to do the long rods. They were ever so long. I had to file the four edges, 'cos when they were new they were very sharp, they'd cut your fingers open. I had to use a square file, a flat file, a smoothing file and then a rep … file on each edge. Then the men who fitted them could handle them. It was hard work. Heavy work. I used to get through the files. One day I had to do twelve rods. I'd managed to do eight by half past five. Then the chargeman came along and said 'haven't you done them yet?' I said 'I've done eight.' He said, 'well you've got four more to do by half past seven.' I said 'you've gotta hope.' He said 'I'll put you on report.' I was cross. I said to my mate 'I've had enough of him, expecting me to do all that lot.' He said to go and see the foreman. So I did. I told him. He said, 'you go back down and just take it easy. I'll sort it out, and he did.'

K.J. Cook writes of a foreman in the blacksmith's shop, who was against having women driving the hammers, and of the boilermaker's representative who pressed for compensation on piece work rates on the grounds that the women would not do the job so well and the men would feel the financial result of this. At the end of the war, however, when the women had to go, Cook says that the men were sorry to lose them saying 'I've never had people earn money for me like them.' Mrs E.P. was on a gang as a rivet-hotter: 'I was on a good gang and got good money … sometimes I got more than my Dad, he wasn't on a good gang. Mind you I worked hard, 'cos I was saving up for my little home … we all were, all us girls. The men were pleased with us, there was no slacking.'

Mrs Alice Coale worked in the 'AM' (machine) shop. She would file down the razor-sharp edges of these long, newly machined locomotive coupling and connecting rods. Despite the GWR issuing free caps to women in the machine shops, in three different colours, to encourage them to cover their hair, few women did. This lady obviously did not, or at least, not for the camera. (Photograph courtesy of the University of Leicester)

Despite their hard work and the proof of their productivity, once the war was over, workshop women had to go. Whilst it is true that most were happy and relieved to do so, given the choice many said they would have loved to have stayed, especially in later years when they looked back over their lives, but the opportunity was denied them. The women's response to this, as expressed by Mrs Vi Joynes, was, as usual, pragmatic: 'We weren't surprised when we had to go as we knew it was only until the men came home. We wouldn't have wanted to keep their jobs from them. That wouldn't have been right, would it?' The reality of the situation, however, was that there was still a staff shortage immediately after the war. Minute 82/47 of 25 March 1947 of the Swindon Branch of the AEU noted that 'a shortage of various sized nuts was causing delays to production. The Locomotive Works manager had placed adverts in the local Press for boys, girls and women to operate the machines in 'R' Shop (the machine shop).' Further Minutes of that year record that 'women are still in the workshops, but in a very limited way'.

Women were still in GWR's Swindon Workshops working on nut-tapping and nut-facing. AEU Minute 104/47.2 states that women over the age of twenty-one who have served the probationary period would receive 90 per cent of the 46s rate; when the railways were nationalised.

1   Penny Summerfield, *Reconstructing Women's Wartime Lives* (1998), p.155.

# CHAPTER 6

# THE STATION

The presence of women in stations was yet another area of difficulty for the GWR and its railwaymen. To understand the dilemma one must appreciate the significance of the station itself, the significance that lies behind the physical façade, for a railway station was more than the sum of its parts; the ticket office, the platforms, the sidings, the signal box. A station was not just a place for trains to pass through or stop at; not just a place for passengers to board and alight, nor just a place for freight to be loaded and unloaded. Neither was it just a place where public and company came together. The station, whether large or small, whilst being all these things, was also the visible face of the Company itself and, as such, was invested with status and authority. As the Company was itself fundamentally masculine, this visible face had need to be the same. The stationmaster, resplendent in his uniform, personified the masculine, hierarchical, conservative railway company. What place then for women? Imagine the difficulty experienced by Company, National and Railway Press as to what to call them! It caused a great deal of consternation. An excellent example of this is a small article run by the *Railway Gazette* on 23 April 1915. Its language highlighted the dilemma:

> A Woman Station *Master*
> Mrs Lidster, daughter of Chief Inspector Lidster of GWR Pontypool commenced duty at Troedyrhew Halt near Merthyr on the GWR & Rhymney Railway. She is the first woman to act in such a capacity in South Wales Another woman is in charge of the Trelwis Junction. Their predecessors in each case have joined the army.

One of the earliest occupations for women on the railways, and one that was not related to domestic skills, was that of crossing keeper and gatewoman or even gate opener, as it was originally known. Gate openers would be employed to open (and shut) the gates onto all kinds of railway property for either workers or vehicles of any sort. Level crossings were primarily introduced to enable carts and animals to cross the early tramroads or wooden wagonways more easily. Gates of various kinds were then introduced. The Liverpool & Manchester Railway preferred gates that went across the public highway barring access to the line and so introduced this practice on their own railway. The Highways Act 1839 required railway level crossings to have gates attended by 'good and proper persons'.[1] The Liverpool & Manchester Railway gates, which were kept closed throughout the day to prevent people and animals straying onto the track during hours of operation, came with bells for summoning the services of the gateman who lived nearby.[2] The gatekeeper on level crossings job was to ensure the gates on level crossings were closed when trains were approaching and passing through, but, at other times, upon request, were opened to accommodate public movement. These gatekeepers, eventually just called crossing keepers, had to work in conjunction with the trains and the nearest signal boxes up and down the line.

Gatekeepers, or gate openers, operated other gates, usually to a company's premises. The earliest gatewoman I have found is a Mrs Corbett at Craven Arms in 1872, who is recorded in the London & North Western and Great Western Joint Railway staff register. A Mrs E. Tipton entered the Company's service in 1876 (no month is recorded) at a wage of 4s per week. In June 1879 a Mrs Newton is also recorded as gatewoman at Ellesmere Port at a wage of just 2s 6d, presumably she was required to open the gates only once or twice a day, in the morning and afternoon. It is also recorded that she was removed in 1880, although no explanation is given. However, one can surmise that it was probably found that her services could be easily dispensed with, or that particular gate was permanently closed. Three years later in September 1882 a Mrs Glover is now at Craven Arms earning 5s per week. It is possible she took over from Mrs Corbett who is then recorded as 'charwoman' from 1881. In February 1884, a Mrs Manning is working at Westbury earning 5s and in November 1887 Mrs Middleton enters at Moreton-on-Lugg also at 5s. These later women are identified as gatekeepers, which became the common usage and was surprisingly deemed politically correct. The same records show that a W. Hampoon, aged twenty-four years, joined in 1858 as a gateman based at Extension at a wage of 18s, which increased in 1877 to 20s, a substantial amount more than any of the women received, but then he may have had to open and shut his gate much more often as well as checking people and vehicles in and out.

The first detailed information regarding female crossing keepers that one comes across is thanks to a 1913 issue of *Railway Magazine*, which carries a small article regarding a Mrs Hill. It seems remarkable that a lowly person such as Mrs Hill has made it onto the pages of such a renowned magazine until one realises that the significance of the article for the male magazine reader is not so much Mrs Hill, but the reputation of the GWR. The magazine, as a voice piece for the railway companies, is pleased to highlight the GWR's magnanimity in allowing Mrs Hill to stay on in the company house and continue in the job, after the death of her husband, which, they write, 'is an act of kindly consideration for which she is deeply grateful'.

The article tells how, after a serious accident in 1880, Mr Hill was transferred to Leigh Wood Crossing, Crowcombe, to assist his recovery. Sadly he never did recover so Mrs Hill 'pluckily undertook his work on the line'. She performed it so well she was allowed to continue after her husband's death. It was a busy job for Mrs Hill, who was 'never absent from her post', dealing with 'ten trains crossing daily in each direction', as well as any 'specials'. At the same time Mrs Hill was bringing up her young family. In time all her children had married and moved away so that she had 'lived alone for thirteen years with no family nearby'. She must have felt very isolated with only the fleeting greetings and waves of the footplate men as they drove past for company and conversation, so imagine how pleased she would have been when one of her daughters came to live nearby. Now, as she told the magazine, she would have 'someone to speak to sometimes'. That small poignant phrase speaks volumes about her loneliness and her working situation. The photograph accompanying the article shows Mrs Hill standing very upright behind the switches of her crossing with one hand on the lever. She looks straight at the camera. One gets the impression of a sound, competent woman, assured in her role however unusual the magazine and the reader might find it.

The public face of the railways had always been masculine, yet Miss Evelyn Derrick, booking clerk, looks relaxed and at home amongst the male staff of Patney & Chirton station, probably it was because she knew them so well – her father was station master. It was an accepted practice, although not common, for this to happen on the GWR, even before the First World War. It had been thought 'an acceptable situation' even back in 1876 when the debate about female clerks began. Evelyn, however, only worked there during the First World War. Front row, left to right: –?–, Station Master John Derrick, Evelyn Derrick, Bert Green, porter. Back row, left to right: –?–, J. Miles, porter, Ernie Cox, signalman, Alec Tilley, porter, George Stone, porter. (Photograph courtesy of David Hyde)

The first detailed information regarding any female crossing/gatekeeper directly from the GWR can be found in the 'Among the Staff' section of the *Magazine* in 1915. It informs that: 'Mrs S.E. Roberts, the level crossing gatekeeper (very mixed terminology) at Vicarage Crossings on the Coed Poeth branch, died on 28th October 1915, at the age of 33 after two days illness. She had been the gatekeeper for 17 years.' The face that looks out from the accompanying photograph is of a bright, pleasant, healthy looking lady. It is a shock to think of her dying so quickly whilst still so young. It is also frustrating to learn so little of her, but it is interesting to note that having been in post for that length of time means she must have started her employment at the age of sixteen years, a seemingly young age for such a responsible job. The next item relating to a female crossing keeper is in the same section, but much later in 1930:

The retirement of Mrs Dyer from Compton Crossing, on October 30th 1930, brought to a close a term of long and faithful service with the company. Mrs Dyer's connection with the crossing went back to the early days of the Didcot, Newbury and Southampton line, for she commenced her duties as crossing keeper two years after the line opened in 1882. There were four gates in those days, and the crossing keeper had to rely entirely on the clock, there being no signals or instruments of any description to assist her. Mrs Dyer remained as crossing keeper there for forty-five years and retired in good health.

Mr Dyer retired in November last year from the permanent way department after forty-five-and-a-half years.

It is good to know that Mrs Dyer has not had to be as lonely in her job as Mrs Hill! Whilst the term gatewoman or crossing keeper was often used as interchangeable, a Census of Staff for 1914 shows that, administratively, the GWR identified them as separate categories. Under the heading 'Female Staff' it categorises crossing keeper (2), whose weekly wages were 20s and 23s and gatewoman (127), with the lowest wage at 2s per week and the highest at 10s 6d, substantially below the crossing keepers reflecting the different levels of responsibility.[3] This handful of women, repeated on other lines too, grew to 705 working as gate or crossing keepers during the First World War. This number continued to increase and in 1934–35; the Railway Year Book records 1,546 female crossing-keepers.

Women workers on the railways were not, as many believe, a First World War innovation. They had been there a long time before that. One such occupation women held was that of crossing keeper. This was a useful means of employment as it came with a house. This one at Compton Crossing looks rather substantial. Mrs Dyer had done the job and lived there for forty-five years. Her connection with the crossing went back to the early days of the Didcot, Newbury and Southampton line. She commenced her duties as crossing keeper just two years after the line opened in 1882. There were four gates in those days, and she had to rely entirely on the clock, there being no signals or instruments of any description to assist her. She retired in 1930.

# Ticket Collectors and Porters

Ticket collectors and porters were two grades in which, after a controversial start, many companies employed women. The GWR's first woman ticket collector, Miss Vera George, was a direct woman. She had had the temerity to write directly to the Company in May 1915, suggesting that 'a woman could be a ticket collector just as well as a man'. The Government and industry were aware of the fact that women were anxious to play their part in the war effort, being pressed by many women's organisations (sixty-eight in London alone) and high profile individuals such as Christabel Pankhurst who was constantly urging them 'to use the women'. The then Prime Minister, Mr Asquith, had already informed the House of Commons in February 1915 that it was 'extremely difficult to fill up the places vacated by [railway] servants who have enlisted'. The *GWR Magazine* of May 1915 reports: 'that there is a desire on the part of women of the country to do all in their power to release men for military service is evident from the numbers who are availing themselves of the special register of women for war service, set up by the Board of Trade'. A banner carried in a women's demonstration through London in the summer of 1915 proclaimed: 'We Demand the Right to Serve'. Such were the sentiments expressed by Miss George when she wrote saying:

> Sir,
>     If you would care to engage me as a ticket collector here, or at any of the smaller stations on the line, and so release a man for more important work, I should be very willing to undertake the duty. I have earned my own living for 10 years, but am now 'unemployed' owing to the war. It struck me that a woman could be a 'ticket collector' just as well as a man.
> Believe me,
> Yours faithfully,
> (Miss) Vera George.

The *Railway Gazette* was not so sure. It wrote in August 1915: 'as porters women must needs be confined to the lighter duties. They are able to act as ticket collectors, though here again some considerable experience will be needed before they are able to perform their work with the assurance of the men they are succeeding.'

Ticket collectors and porters were very visible posts. Unlike clerical work or jobs in workshops these positions were very much in the public eye. Not only that, women in these posts would be expected to exert authority over the travelling public, including male passengers. How could traditionally subservient women handle such roles? The *Railway Review* of June 1915 expressed its concerns saying: 'The ticket collector is often exposed to the calumnies of a rough element which passes through the ticket gates and this is the objectionable part of the position, unsuitable to the fair sex.' The NUR also had great difficulty believing that women could do the job. They produced a series of cartoons *When Women Take the Place of Men on the Railway* in their union magazine *The Railway Review*. Those of July/August 1915 depict the new female ticket collector in sexually provocative clothing (rather than the railway uniforms the women were by this time wearing) being ogled by an 'older' gentleman and being challenged by a drunk. The female porter is shown wearing high-fashion Edwardian dress and feathered hat, tottering in her buttoned-up boots, hanging on to her handbag and fixing her face-powder whilst looking into her hand-held mirror, this despite urgent warnings from the passenger – whose luggage she is supposed to be delivering – that 'the train's just going!' Indeed, it was a huge leap of faith for society to take on board that women were physically up to jobs such as ticket collecting or as porters, let alone mentally or emotionally. Up to the beginning of the war, society's construction

Miss Vera George, the GWR's first female ticket collector, resplendent in her uniform. She led the way to new employment for women on the GWR.

of women, i.e. how women were perceived to be, was still based on fundamental concepts laid down centuries before. Women were seen in terms of opposites to men: so as man was strong, women was, therefore, weak or at least frail, or, if you were middle or upper class 'delicate'. Men were considered rational, intellectual beings, but women were not. Women were emotional, which made them suitable for caring and nurturing but also irrational, which in turn made them unsuitable to have the vote! Men were the protectors and providers so women must be in need of protection and provision; man as the provider was in the workplace; woman as the carer was in the home. Boys were brought up and educated to know this and so were girls. What education they had reflected this status quo, so, when the GWR and railway magazines constantly referred to 'the gentler sex' or 'the fair sex' or 'the weaker sex', they were merely reflecting society's patriarchal, paternalistic attitude to women. Of course, this was an umbrella approach and it could not possibly be applied as a 'one-coat-covers-all'. In reality, millions of women were already in the workplace – the *War Cabinet Report on Women in Industry* shows that in 1914, 5.9 million women were 'gainfully employed' – as single and married women, either full or part time, working class and middle class, and they were there because their earnings were essential to their own or their family's income. Many were also doing heavy, physical work; women had been employed in the coal mines, in the mills and working on the land decades before this; their work as domestic servants was no picnic either; so the words of *The Railway Gazette* in June 1917 hit the spot when they wrote: 'That they should successfully undertake work calling for such severe physical endurances as the work of porters in railway goods sheds is a possibility which would have been simply derided three years ago.'

The NUR obviously found this public appearance of railwaywomen disturbing for many reasons, not least that the public were being made aware of the fact that women were earning their own incomes. The unions had fought a long and bitter fight to get decent pay for working men and had negotiated on the basis of a family wage. Women, single and married, earning a separate income could place this arrangement in jeopardy. The NUR saw the war period as an opportunity to bargain hard and obtain concessions for their male members, yet at the same time feminists such as Eleanor Rathbone and Millicent Fawcett were also pushing if not for equal pay for equal work then for a new and better formula such as equal pay for equal results, thereby adding to the NUR's anxieties. Despite the NUR's obvious worries and open hostility, the need for women railway workers was an unforgiving reality and the union, like Canute, found it could not stem the tide and in July 1915 had to formally acknowledge women railway workers by agreeing, somewhat reluctantly, to their membership of the union. By 1918 the GWR, although similarly reluctant, had taken on 323 women ticket collectors, 346 female porters and 616 female goods porters.

Because of the initial belief that the war would be short-lived – over by Christmas – the women were not immediately issued with any railway clothing or uniforms at the beginning of their employment. Women made do and fashioned garments to suit the occupation. Engine cleaners found it much easier to adopt male attire and took to wearing trousers. Daringly, photographs appeared in railway magazines showing women in these very provocative outfits. In the general course of things all of this would have been extremely shocking, challenging social morality codes, but, because it was in aid of the war effort it was portrayed as not only practical and sensible, protecting women's modesty, but also as respectable and patriotic. Interestingly, no such photos appeared in the *GWR Magazine*, only ones of appropriately dressed female employees. As the war dragged on, however, it became apparent that women would be necessary for a much longer period than at first anticipated. The companies were anxious to maintain standards and discipline which the uniforms helped to enforce, so it became desirable and necessary to put female employees into appropriate versions of those worn by the men. Uniforms were issued throughout the companies and much comment and propaganda was made of it, with articles and photographs appearing in company magazines and the railway and national press. The *GWR Magazine* shows a splendidly smart Miss George resplendent in her ticket collector's uniform.

During the Second World War the novelty of women in uniform, especially on the railways, had not disappeared and once again the railway magazines were keen to display 'members of the fair sex', suitably booted and suited. As before, however, there was still the need to reassure society, men and the Company that these women were still 'womanly'. Collie Knox writes of the GWR women: 'What is so remarkable about our women at war is that although they have poured themselves into uniforms of every colour shape and size, they have contrived still to remain essentially women.'

During the Second World War large numbers of women were taken on by the railways for 'porterage' duties, or, to announce it in the grander tones used by the GWR: 'For the second time during the century the withdrawal of man power from the Railways to meet the war requirements of the Services, has necessitated the employment of women as porters.' Despite the examples of women's ability as porters in the First World War, and despite this being recognised by many – Edwin Pratt wrote: 'women wheeled heavily laden trucks with great pride and would never admit that men could do any work better than they could do it themselves' – the GWR still harboured concerns and lack of belief. James Milne, GWR general manager, declared: 'to assist women porters in handling traffic, an appeal is to be made to government departments,

Society was worried about the ability of women to cope with the travelling public, and particularly with difficult male passengers, but the women proved adept and capable and the GWR eventually employed 323 female ticket collectors during the First World War.

Some G.W.R. war-time workers—restaurant car waitresses and ticket collectors.

During the First World War women were taken on as temporary substitutes for men who had signed up with the Armed Services and they could be seen working on trains and in stations. Here we see restaurant-car waitresses and ticket collectors, the top picture being of Miss Vera George, the GWR's first female ticket collector.

Tickets please! Having established that women could do the job in the First World War, the Second World War saw even more employed in this capacity, close-up and confident with the travelling public. (Photograph courtesy of the University of Leicester)

Railway police had exactly the same authority and powers of arrest as the general police. GWR policewoman P. Mitchell, going about her duty at Bristol Temple Meads station in February 1942. The first GWR policewoman at Plymouth, Mrs Lilian Gale, was killed whilst on duty when knocked down in the docks by an engine. (Photograph courtesy of the University of Leicester)

Being a policewoman seemed an attractive proposition to women in the Second World War. The *GWR Magazine* (1941) tells how an advertisement for a single vacancy attracted 300 applications. At that time fifty policewomen had been employed on the GWR; here one of them deals with two small evacuees. (Photograph courtesy of the University of Leicester)

traders and the public, to restrict the weight of packages, including luggage.' The *Magazine* later argued that this plea for lighter parcels was a 'gallant' one out of respect for 'the weaker sex'.

At this time, 1941, loss of man power on the railways was beginning to bite as war demands on its services grew even heavier, however, women's participation in the war effort was still voluntary – conscription for women between the ages of twenty and thirty years was not brought in until December 1942 – and so the GWR was keen to couch its encouragement and praise in patriotic terms declaring: 'a desire to perform work of national importance seems to have permeated the fair sex, as the response to the Great Western Railway appeal for women workers has on the whole been good'. It is upbeat in its article 'Wartime Women Employees' reporting that: 'Girls who have undertaken porterage duties in country stations have had special attention focused upon them.' It tells of Miss Freda M. Jones who has 'achieved friendly notoriety in the district immediately surrounding Pontdolgoch … as the "Pooh Bah" of the railway station'. Freda performed 'all essential duties, including the issue and collection of tickets, the booking of parcels, and the giving of "right-away" for trains' and 'like her predecessor before her, she works under the supervision of the stationmaster at an adjoining station'. What is a 'Pooh Bah'? Presumably a 'jack-of-all-trades'. The novelty value of such girls helped glamorise the job and assist recruitment. Mr Keith Steele who joined the GWR in 1945 as a train recorder in Birmingham South signal box has clear memories of a number of women in the stations along the line between Birmingham and Wolverhampton. Keith distinctly remembers his very first encounter with a railwaywoman, when he was introduced to Lil Brown, a ticket collector at Snow Hill station. He particularly remembers the female porters at Biltson G.W. He writes: 'Snow, hail or rain, of which we had a lot during those winters, you could always rely on the

In 1941 this photograph appeared in the *GWR Magazine* with the caption: 'We reproduce a photograph of Miss Florence Hibbott, who makes a pleasing and efficient looking picture with her luggage barrow at Buttington station.' It goes on to say: 'In all, more than 8,000 members of *the fair sex* are now working on the Great Western Railway.'

*Left:* Thelma Hoare and Doreen Stevens as they were then, worked as porters doing 'all the things the men did, bar the sheeting of the wagons', at Steventon station before going on to be signalwomen.

*Below:* Daisy Jewell worked as a porter at Pensford station in 1942 where her sister Mary was the signalwoman. They were the station master's first experience of working with females. Such was their 'novelty' that they both appeared in a feature about women on the railways, in their local paper.

Woman power! A female porter skilfully draws a fully loaded parcels barrow across the concourse in Paddington goods station. (Photograph courtesy of the University of Leicester)

women at Bilston G.W, Violet Jones (transferred from Swan Village), Rosana Pritchard and Marie Watson. When on nights in the box you could guarantee seeing them opening up the station 4 a.m. sharp to meet the fish train. They would unload boxes and boxes of fish for Bilston Market. The signalman would leave the box to assist in pushing the loaded barrows across the barrow ramp and onto the opposite platform ready for collection by the cartage man.' Keith also remembers there were several female family members at different stations. Violet Jones' mother, Mrs Holmes worked at Bilston West Midland with Marie Rhodes, whilst Marie's two sisters, Dolly and Florence worked at Wednesbury station.

Mrs Ruth Newton, born Ruth Cuss, always wanted to work on the railway. She was probably influenced by the many hours she spent in the signal box with her father, George. George Cuss was a signalman in the Lower Heyford station box, situated between Banbury and Oxford, and Ruth would often refuse to go to church on Sunday evenings to spend more time with him there. 'You can't work on the railways,' Ruth's father would say, 'They don't have ladies on the railway.' One day Ruth came home all excited. She had seen a lady working on Oxford railway station. 'See Dad, they do have ladies on the railways,' she said. 'Doing what, though?' he asked. 'Looking after the toilets,' she said. 'You don't want to do that love, do you?' The poor man was bewildered and horror struck. In truth Ruth was so 'mad on the railways,' to quote Ron, her husband, she would have done almost anything to work there, so she was absolutely thrilled, and her father very relieved, when she got the opportunity to do so during the war.

In 1941, aged eighteen, an exuberant Ruth started as a porter in Heyford station. Her family lived in Heyford village so Ruth already knew many of the station workers and the stationmaster, Mr Wimlet, as well as many local passengers. Ruth settled in happily, having no trouble with working the two shifts, early morning and late afternoon. It was a very busy job mainly due to

These small 'Mercury Mechanical Horses' used to be commonplace in the railway stations, as was the parcel traffic which is obviously being dealt with here. Many women, who had never driven anything mechanical before, learnt to drive a variety of motorised machines during their wartime work on the railways. (Photograph courtesy of the University of Leicester)

A battery-powered, flat-bed mechanised horse with a 'string of barrows' laden with parcels and urgent goods which in those 'far off days' always went by passenger train. Note that the rear two coaches are in the wartime all-over brown livery while the nearer coach retains the traditional chocolate and cream which will always be associated with the GWR. (Photograph courtesy of the University of Leicester)

the fact that there was an RAF station at Upper Heyford about a mile from Lower Heyford. Her many duties included attending to parcel traffic, cleaning and filling signal lamps for the visiting lamp man, sweeping the platform and collecting tickets from passengers. She also had to help the male goods porter with the heavier goods in the station yard, stacking cereals, potatoes and boxes of goods such as vegetables. In those days country shops were serviced by goods brought in daily or weekly by train and then delivered from the station by the company lorry and driver based there, so the porters were kept extremely busy. After about 6 p.m. on her afternoon shifts she would be alone at the station mainly collecting tickets. Her final duty around 11 p.m. was to meet the last train from Oxford. She then had to lock up the station.

During her time at Heyford, Ruth got to know many of the servicemen passing through her station, so it was extremely distressing and traumatic for her to have to deal with the coffins that arrived from the RAF station with bodies of air crew who had been killed in operational or training flying duties. Two of the air crew she got to know well, Scotsmen Bill Nicol and 'Jock' McKay, would always wait for her to finish locking up, and, as the camp road passed Ruth's house, they would walk her home. Tragically Bill was killed at Heyford in a flying mishap and Ruth had the devastating job of addressing the coffin to his home at Lanark. When Jock McKay was later shot down in a Lancaster bomber over Germany, the RAF kindly informed Ruth of his death.

Unexpectedly, after learning the job and proving very useful in it, for some reason Ruth was transferred from Heyford to Leamington Spa, Warwickshire. The family believe it was because 'it was felt it would be bad for morale, as it wasn't done for young single girls to stay at home when so many were being sent off all over the country for the war effort.' Strangely enough Ruth's married sister, Alice Stockley, who had to return to the family home in Heyford with

Mrs Ruth Newton (*née* Cuss) always wanted to work on the railway and was thrilled when the Second World War gave her the chance to do so. First she was a porter at Lower Heyford and then a guard at Leamington Spa. Here she is at Lower Heyford with her father George Cuss, who was a signalman.

her husband when their house in Swanage was bombed, went to work in Heyford station as a booking clerk and her husband as a porter. A brother-in-law of Ruth's sister Mary also worked as a porter at Heyford station after Ruth left. Perhaps he took her place!

An area of porterage not as well known and one of the more unusual tasks undertaken by women was that of the female travelling porter. In 1943 the GWR had eighty-five such positions. They were stationed all over the system in Paddington, Bath, Birkenhead, Bristol, Cardiff, Carmarthen, Chester, Didcot, Exeter, Hereford, Newport (Monmouthshire) Newton Abbott, Oxford, Pembroke, Plymouth, Shrewsbury, Swansea, Swindon, Taunton, Trowbridge, Westbury (Wiltshire), Weymouth, Whitland, Wolverhampton and Worcester. Every day they would travel sweeps of up to 250 train miles over several counties before returning to base. These girls formed their parcels 'flying squad'. This squad was part of the Company's 'intensified campaign to combat wartime pressures of traffic volume and staff shortages' and 'to avert delays due to over-carrying, short-carrying and mis-transfers'. These porters had a very precise job, with precise objectives and a definitive set of outcomes. The article 'GWR Women Travelling Porters' explains it exactly:

> Their special duty is to see that every package loaded at the starting station and everywhere else *en route*, goes into the right van on the right train, in the exact spot in that van to suit the destination, so that the pile of parcels for each place lies handy by the most convenient door, ready to be whisked out the moment the train stops.

The article then outlines the porter's daily routine:

> Each girl first directs the loading of the traffic at her 'home' station into the out going train. Then she hops into the guard's van and goes on tour, working in turn for each of the twenty or thirty stationmasters at whose platforms the train may stop. She also does a lot of work during the journey, making necessary adjustments to the stowage of the load, passing from van to van through the connecting gangsways.
>
> There is no guess work about this sorting. Special training has made her a travelling gazetteer of the line, with a quick answer for almost any query as to the proper parking-spot for a particular parcel.
>
> In addition she helps speed the train by calling out the station names, by closing doors and by helping in a score of other ways.

This area of railway history is sadly bereft of detail and this short article is a goldmine of information about one set of railwaywomen's working lives. It is pure treasure and pleasure! The GWR are obviously delighted with the outcomes of this initiative as it goes on in an almost effusive manner:

> The travelling girl porter is the 'good fairy' of all the calling stations, especially the one-man wayside stops where her pair of expert hands actually doubles the station's staff strength… Already the timekeeping of over 300 of the busiest regular trains has been improved by the 'flying squad'.

These are the most fulsome and supportive words written by the GWR in regard to their female employees that I have come across. No comparisons of standards in respect to men are made. No female frailties are highlighted. Nothing implies that they might fall down on the job and there is no hint of a suggestion that they need male supervision to operate efficiently. Here the women travelling porters are identified as trained, expert, self regulating and delivering good

*Above:* A travelling porter sorts and stows the various goods in their exact place and in exact order for quick unloading at the correct destination. (Photograph courtesy of the University of Leicester)

*Right:* Part of a guard's essential equipment were the flags (red and green) and the whistle used to see off the train. This guard is identified as Mrs N. James, first woman guard doing regular duty on express trains between London and Gloucester. (Photograph courtesy of the University of Leicester)

results, albeit whilst being addressed as 'girls' which they may have 'legally' been. Incidentally, a last little item of information given is that altogether the girls travel more than 12,000 miles a day, equal to half way round the world!

## Guards

The job of a guard was another traditionally male job that women began to do. It was a very responsible job as it required one to issue commands regarding the movement of the train. With a blow on the whistle and wave of the flag one would set a train in motion. All guards were issued with a set of equipment necessary to carry out their duties and they were required to look after them and keep them clean. A guard's equipment included:

> Watch; whistle; carriage key; set of flags (red and green); hand lamp; rule book; general appendix; service time books; local appendices; weekly train and special notices; wrong line orders; 12 Detonators.

The twelve detonators, which were also carried by the fireman, were in case the train became parted or broken down on a section in between signal boxes. The fireman had to go forward and place a detonator on the opposite track – one at quarter of a mile, one at half a mile and three at three quarters of a mile. The guard had to do the same behind the nearest part of the train and on the track it was stood on. Keith Steele remembers one guard whose hand lamp was legendary. Dolly Whittaker and Jean Turley were passenger guards at Wolverhampton. Jean was nicknamed 'the Glamour Guard', as she was always immaculately turned out; trousers neatly pressed, brass buttons and shoes polished and shiny and always a buttonhole in her lapel. Jean polished her hand lamp so much she cleaned it of all the black paint, then burnished it until it shone like silver.

Ruth Newton had initially worked as a porter at Heyford station, but for unrevealed reasons, she was transferred to another station away from home, yet when she got there Ruth found that they did not seem to need her. No one knew what to do with her. They had not actually asked for anyone. She was very unhappy. Living in digs and just hanging about filling in during the day did not seem like a worthwhile war effort! It was fortunate that Mr Harry Gwyn, a traffic inspector, visited the station and, happily, he knew Ruth and her father, George, personally. He enquired as to her welfare and Ruth told him. Unfortunately, it had been decreed by those in charge that Ruth should go to Leamington Spa and so there she had to stay, but Mr Gwyn had her transferred on to guard duties and so Ruth got to travel on the trains up and down the line.

In her new official little black guard's notebook, Ruth kept a note of all her equipment, new duties, responsibilities and relevant information that a guard needed to know, such as:

> A list of all the train times on the up line and down line from Leamington Spa.
> The weight and wheel requirements for passenger trains.
> All of the signal boxes and telephone boxes along her stretch of line – in case of emergencies.
> Information regarding milk tanks, cattle wagons, Sunday specials and other technical specifications.

One of the new duties that Ruth enjoyed more than any other was when she had to accompany a special train to Great Aln, which is near Bearley on the Stratford and Leamington line. At first she was not allowed on this duty because she only had a skirt with her uniform and it was a vital

Left luggage or lost property? Everything and anything from tin helmet, suitcase or canvas sack, had to be labelled, sorted and stowed away to be easily retrievable when requested. Women of more mature years were often given this lighter work. (Photograph courtesy of the University of Leicester)

requirement that she wore trousers, but once the trousers arrived, she was off. The special train was made up of just one coach and a push-and-pull engine, a 0-4-2 of 48XX/14XX class. Ron, Ruth's husband, remembers her telling him how 'smart business- type people would get on with their cases and bags and sit in silence for the whole journey'. When they got to the destination the passengers disembarked but the coach would be uncoupled and left there. Ruth had to travel back on the footplate, hence the need for trousers which were obviously to protect her modesty when clambering up and down to the footplate but also offered some protection from the scorching heat of the firebox. For Ruth, travelling on the footplate along with the driver and the fireman was such a thrill. What a privilege and one that few women experienced. Later on the same day, the engine would return to Great Alne with another guard (Ruth would be off duty) and pick up these secret people. It all seemed very strange and hush hush. The railway staff believed it to be part of the 'behind-the-scenes' war effort, so did not ask too much.

Ruth also worked on suburban passenger trains of four or eight coaches which stopped at all stations to Birmingham and Wolverhampton, and a much longer train, about ten corridor coaches, which stopped at all the stations between Stratford-on-Avon, Worcester, the suburbs of Birmingham and into Snow Hill, Birmingham. Sometimes Ruth would be on duty on the last train going from Leamington Spa to Fenny Compton, which was put on to convey soldiers back to their camp after an evening out in the town. Some, who'd had a few too many, would behave in a disorderly manner. The drivers on these trains told Ruth not to look along the train when it was moving as many of the men would relieve themselves out of an opened door or window. At Fenny Compton a lot would leap out, not onto the platform, but onto the opposite track, and then run off; they were the ones without tickets or passes. Despite this behaviour, Ruth, personally, never had any problems with them. Roy used to tease her and tell her she was not pretty enough, especially wearing trousers. Obviously many still then thought that trousers were not a feminine way to dress! Ruth then travelled back to Leamington Spa on the last local train, booked off at midnight and walked the half mile home, many times in the blackout.

Like many wartime railwaywomen, Ruth met her husband through work. Roy joined the GWR at Llantrisant in 1941, as an engine cleaner. Just after promotion to fireman he was sent, on the day of his seventeenth birthday, to Leamington Spa. One day fate played a helping hand. Roy and his driver, Fred Rees, got to travel back from a job with Ruth in the guard's van of her train. They sat on mail bags, sharing Roy's very precious bag of cherries. Roy asked Ruth out. They were married in September 1946. Ruth did not leave work immediately on her marriage, but stayed on until she was expecting her first child in 1947.

1  'The Oxford Companion to British Railway History.
2  Ibid.
3  Census of Staff 1914. David Hyde Collection.

# CHAPTER 7

# THE SIGNAL BOX

Signal boxes, like the engine cab, were sacred male dominions. It was a job that carried immense responsibility. In the early days of railway signalling the track was divided into sections, which were patrolled and protected by special constables who became known as 'Bobbies'. These constables were also expected to give notice of obstructions and safely control the movement of the railway traffic. To enable them to stay nearby and guard the track they had track-side station houses or shelters. Eventually the constables' duties changed to the prevention of crime and signalmen became the ones with the duty of safety and of controlling traffic movements. The function of the station houses changed to signal boxes. The nickname 'Bobby' stayed with the signalmen. The men who worked the boxes were looked up to and respected. In normal times a man had to work hard and put in the years to get one. The work history of William Frederick Higgins, dated 26 June 1931 and prepared by GWR's Divisional Superintendent's Office, Gloucester, illustrates this perfectly. William Higgins, No. 59472, was born 26 March 1898. His record states that between joining in June 1914 and leaving to join the army in December 1916, he went from lad porter, to porter, to goods porter Cl.4, working at three different stations at wages from 15s per week to 18s. He rejoined the GWR in May 1919 as signal porter at Brymbo station and went through various other grades before moving to Rhos as porter signalman, then temporary signalman, before eventually becoming signalman Cl.5 at Drwsynant in September 1927 earning 51s per week. Along the way he achieved several signalling and ambulance certificates. When he was made redundant in 1931 he was still signalman Cl.5, but earning only 50s. William Henry Hulme, on the other hand, had a helping hand from staff difficulties in the First World War. He joined in March 1913 as a goods porter and just two months later became a porter. In June 1914 he was signal porter and became a signalman in December 1918.[1] During the Second World War apart from the grade of porter-signalmen, there were seven classes of signalmen in the services. The job was a whole lot more than just 'keeping the lever brasses clean and shiny' and knowing when and how to pull them, although all these parts were considered essential. One had also to learn the codes, bells and block systems and monitoring the all important tail-lamp. The signal box was, therefore, like the engine cab, considered sacrosanct against the invasion of female war recruits. The unions and the railwaymen, no matter how desperate or difficult the times were, no matter which company they worked for, were unanimous in their opposition to women being given posts of such responsibility. Company magazines as well as the Railway Press all carried articles highlighting the folly of such thinking. The NUR's *Railway Review* (August 1918) declared that 'lever-pulling is not good for women's delicate constitution'.

Despite all this there was one notable woman who had in 1890, by fair means or foul, managed to work her way into a small GWR box situated midway between Brampton and Morebath, near the Somerset border with Devon. She was brought to public attention by the *Daily Telegraph* where it was picked up by a 1913 issue of *The Railway Magazine*. It tells of Mrs Town: 'She has satisfactorily discharged the duties of her position for twenty-three years, and lives in a semi-detached cottage near the signal box, her daughter being her only companion. There are seven trains daily in each direction, except on Friday (market day) when the number is slightly increased' and finishes with: 'Mrs Town is very proud of her work.' Rightly so. It would appear that Mrs Town may well have been, not only the first GWR woman to work in one of its signal boxes, but also the only GWR woman to make a career out of it.

All through the First World War railwaymen resisted the employment of women in signal boxes pledging themselves to do all in their power to prevent it on the grounds of safety – the safety of the public and the safety of the women. They also pointed out the unsuitability of the work for women or women for the work.[2] It has to be said that not all the men who made it to signalmen were suitable for the job either. The staff registers with work records are full of instances when signalmen had to be taken to task or disciplined for behaviour 'unsuited' to the job such as 'leaving the box for natural purposes and omitting to take off his signals after accepting L6 for 8.15 p.m'., 'cautioned for not properly setting the points – resulting in wagon becoming derailed', and even 'dismissed for going to sleep whilst on duty'.[3] Somewhat surprisingly, *The Railway Gazette* of August 1917 ran an article which actually praised the women, saying that they were 'capable of safely and satisfactorily meeting all the emergencies that a signal box creates and furnishes'. Little information can be found of women who worked in GWR's signal boxes during the First World War but a very small article in the *Magazine* of December 1919 does identify one. It states: 'Among the women wartime workers on the GWR was Mrs Emily C. Rowles, who took charge of the signal box at Dymock station from June 1918 up to last month.' Edwin Pratt's book gives figures for the First World War women working in 'Signal' but not what and where. He wrote: 'although the companies themselves considered that the women were equal to the work, the men in the signal boxes alongside were apt to raise objections and declare that "they could not accept the responsibility".'

It is no surprise then that when the Second World War came along the situation had changed little, men and unions still thought that women into signal boxes did not go. An article in the *Daily Telegraph* in October 1942 under the heading: 'Rail Jobs Women Cannot Do' stated: 'many jobs could be done only by fully trained men. The heavier work of shunters and signalmen is beyond a woman's capacity.' Appraising the situation later in 1947 in regard to the Southern Railway, Bernard Darwin writes of a district inspector who taught the women signalling. This inspector found the women 'rather superficial and impatient of grounding in principles ... they were not very good at textbooks and regulations and official language'. Darwin, however, points out what many other commentators preferred to overlook, that the teaching of the women 'depended on the skilled men who had been kept at home' subtly raising questions regarding the standard of instruction, i.e. of the men.

During the Second World War the Collingbourne Dulcis signal box on the old Midland & South Western Junction Railway section of the GWR, was home to several of this new breed of signal*men*, here three young teenage girls, Peggy, Doreen and Thelma, learned new skills, enjoyed new experiences and played their part in keeping Britain's railways rolling during the time of national crisis.

Peggy Baber (*née* Ruddle) couldn't wait to do her bit for the war. Her two elder sisters had already left home, one to the WRAF and one to the ATS and Peggy used to joke that if the war

Many women interviewed said that working on the railways during the Second World War was 'the best time of my life'. This lady, Florence 'Duck' Sainsbury, looks as if it was. On a warm summer's day in 1941, shown still in uniform having just finished her shift in Seend signal box, Florence stops off at The Brewery Inn, a regular calling place on her way home from work. The Seend signal box was a Class 5 and worked on a two-shift basis, from 6.00 a.m. to 2.00 p.m. and 2.00 p.m to 10 p.m. so presumably Florence had been on the early shift. (Photograph courtesy of Greta Buckland)

had not ended before she could join up, she would enlist with the WRENS. Her father, Arthur Ruddle, who had been a special-class signalman before disability caused him to take a posting as crossing keeper at Crofton Crossing where Peggy was born, had different ideas and told Peggy to join the railway. Like a dutiful daughter of the time, she did.

Word on the railway grapevine had it that they were going to allow girls into signal boxes at just seventeen and a half years old. The idea of being a signalwoman excited Peggy. She took herself off to her nearest local box on the main line – previously closed down but re-opened and operating around the clock seven days a week to cope with the war traffic – and persuaded the three, rather young, signalmen, two local lads Cyril Harding and Jimmy Hilliard, and Billy Froud from Yetminster, to teach her the rules and regulations, bill codes and how a signal box was laid out. Suitably prepared, she was off to a flying start. She took the oral test and Holmgren's test for colour-blindness which used coloured wools to test 'the power of distinguishing shades of green, pink and red' with Divisional Inspector Wilmot at Bristol and easily passed. In 1942 at the age of seventeen years and eight months, just over the legal age to sign up for war work, Peggy joined the railway and became a signalwoman. This would have seemed totally unbelievable to railwaymen in general but even more so to those in this particular job. They would have had to climb 'the ladder of promotion' like William Higgins. For them it was a bad enough situation with very young lads coming in and being 'made-up' so quickly, so it is easy to imagine and even understand their annoyance when young women were 'bounced into the job' to use the words of Doreen Stevens, one of the 'Jenny-come-lately' signalwomen. On top of all of this, these women were still merely girls, under the legal age to be described as woman or adult; the legal age one attained adulthood then being twenty-one. No wonder there was resentment and resistance, but the country's need was greater than the maintaining of accepted practices and male pride and so Peggy entered the signal box.

She took naturally to the job and just six months later she was back at Bristol for re-testing after further training for moving up to the 'bit more complicated', although still class 5 box at Grafton & Burbage. Once again Mr Wilmot had every confidence in her ability and suggested that she just 'go on and enjoy yourself'. She did, as she loved the job.

Whilst Peggy had passed all the oral exams required of her, there had been no requirement for any theoretical or written work, indeed there was no obligation for any further study or exams as she was now as qualified as she was required to be. However, Peggy, and her good friend Doreen, decided to extend their knowledge and expertise and study for the railway signalling exam. Each week, for a number of weeks they were sent papers from the Swindon office on a specific related subject to study, which included revision questions for practice written answers. At the end they had to travel to Swindon for a final written exam, marked out of 500 points. The pass mark was 250 points. They both passed. 300 points was a 'merit' pass. Peggy achieved 292. Her father was really disappointed on her behalf but Peggy was pleased that she had done so well. The only official acknowledgement or reward she got for this achievement was a certificate and 'being granted a day off to go to Swindon to sit the exam', yet at the time, this exam was a stepping stone on the career path for a signalman seeking promotion and for a would-be station master. One of the criticisms levelled at women in both world wars was that they lacked ambition and motivation and that they did not seek further responsibility or advancement. This was obviously not the case for these two women. They also proved that they were 'very good at textbooks and regulations and official language'.

Peggy's fondest signal-box memory was coming face to face with armed men! Having come on night shift she was informed by the departing signalman that there were 'some manoeuvres going on out there'. Getting on with the work, Peggy thought little more of it. Some time later a train in her section had to stop as it did not have the line ahead clear. According to Rule 55, the guard on the stopped train came down to enquire the reason for the wait. Once she was able to inform him that they now 'had the line' the guard would take off back to his train. Sometimes, unfortunately, the man would miss jumping aboard the now moving train and it was not at all unusual for him to return to the box somewhat red faced, therefore, on hearing footsteps coming up the steps, Peggy expected an embarrassed guard. She turned grinning just as three American servicemen armed with revolvers, pointing straight at her, stepped inside the box. Each were as shocked as the other. Peggy because there had been a recent murder of a young local girl by an American serviceman and the servicemen because they, as the officer later explained, had been expecting a man, not a pretty, young girl. The Americans, who, to use their words, had been 'larking about expecting to give some bobby a fright', were extremely apologetic. They were so concerned for Peggy's distress that they stayed with her until she had gotten over the shock and all were able to laugh about the matter.

Peggy hated having to leave the box, she had enjoyed it so much. In 1994 there was some debate in the *Railnews* magazine as to who had been the youngest signalwoman during the war. Peggy was able to furnish the evidence, very convincingly, that it was her.

Mrs Doreen Stevens (*née* Spackman) and Mrs Thelma Durnford (*née* Hoare) had been friends since childhood. They lived in the same street opposite each other. They went to the same schools together and they went into the railways together. At first they were employed as porters

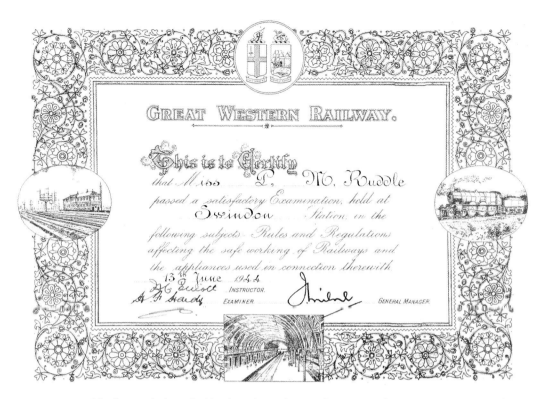

GREAT WESTERN RAILWAY.

This is to Certify

that Miss P. M. Ruddle

passed a satisfactory Examination, held at

Swindon Station, in the

following subjects Rules and Regulations

affecting the safe working of Railways and

the appliances used in connection therewith

13th June 1944

INSTRUCTOR.

A. F. Hardy EXAMINER.

GENERAL MANAGER.

Peggy Ruddle (later Baber) worked hard to obtain this certificate, narrowly missing a 'merit' pass. This was not a requirement for her work, she did it purely for her own satisfaction.

at Steventon station under Mr Ellis the station master and were stationed there for nearly two years. In that time they did all the usual porter duties. 'We did the same jobs as the men,' says Doreen 'except for sheeting the wagons. We loaded the trucks and unloaded goods for RAF Harwell.' When they wanted to avoid Mr Ellis, they would hide away in the marshalling yard. Here they would enjoy watching the men shunting. Shunting, like signal work, was another area thought beyond women's capabilities and was one of the last areas to admit female workers. Shunting is the procedure whereby individual wagons are marshalled together to make up one goods train which is going to a specific destination. For example, Train A would be made up of two wagons of hay, two wagons of milk containers, three wagons of coal, one wagon of fruit and vegetables all to go to South Wales. Meanwhile, Train B bound for Bristol was made up of four wagons of coal, four wagons of hay and two wagons of fruit and vegetables. The wagons were uncoupled from a run of trucks of one commodity, shunted onto the right railroad or sidings, where the train is being made up and then coupled together. The coupling and uncoupling are achieved by means of a long pole with a hook. It is difficult work and can be dangerous, which is why rules and procedures are applied. Like many railway jobs it requires a 'knack' and team work between the shunter, head shunter and engine driver. Whilst Doreen was impressed by the shunting, she was less than impressed when the men forgot procedure and 'fly-shunted' instead. This was an illegal practice, but one that was common in marshalling yards all over the country because it saved a great deal of time. In shunting, every wagon is pushed or shunted all the way by the engine on to the right railroad, but in fly-shunting, after the initial shunt, the wagon goes or flies on its own. On top of which, once the wagons had buffered together a man would have

These three women loved their time as signal women. Front row, left to right: Doreen Stevens (*née* Spackman) here, at the time of the photograph, working in the booking office at Savernake station, Peggy Baber (*née* Ruddle) who popped in for a visit on her day off from working in Grafton-Burbage box and Thelma Durnford (*née* Hoare) working in Collingbourne box. Back row, left to right: Arty Stroud, porter; Station Master Millard and -?- shunter.

to squeeze in between them and put on the coupling loop by hand. To men who had spent years of their lives shunting, had developed the pole techniques and the muscles in the midriff that came with it, and who had also developed the casual attitude that comes with familiarity of the work, it came easily, but to young teenage girls new to the job and the world of railways, it was a frightening and dangerous spectacle. It is not surprising that Doreen preferred the security and orderliness of the signal box. One of Doreen's duties as a porter was taking a turn to work a farm crossing box, especially during harvest time:

> Once I was asked to take my uncle's turn in the Causeway crossing box so he could take his annual leave, as there was no relief man available. That gave me a taste for the signal box, so when the district inspector asked if I would take a post as a signal woman, I jumped at the chance and went to Collingbourne.

Doreen loved working in the signal box. She took to it like a duck to water. It did not matter that in the beginning she had to work twelve-hour shifts; it did not matter that every time she needed the loo she had wait until there was enough time to go down the steps, across the line and into the station and along to the toilet, hoping it would not be engaged by a passenger, and then

Doreen Stevens (*née* Spackman) and her friend Thelma Durnford (*née* Hoare) in their signal box at Collingbourne Dulcis at change-over time. One had a good view from the box and Doreen remembers that one night she saw a long row of little lights advancing up the track. It was the Home Guard out on patrol with glow worms on their hats to light the way!

have enough time to make the return journey back again. It did not matter that such enormous responsibility rested on her young shoulders, to her it was simply 'the best time of my life. I could have stayed there forever'. Her signal box with its little stove with stackpipe that provided heat and an oven for warming something up and a place to boil the kettle for a good brew – an important tradition in all signal boxes – was her pride and joy. 'It was hard work,' says Doreen, 'especially on frosty, cold mornings with the distant signal 1,575 yards away. We had lots of troop trains, including the ambulance trains from Southampton after the D-Day landings coming through, as well as ammunition trains from the Midlands to Southampton for the army at Tidworth and goods traffic to and from the Army Medical Centre at Everleigh. We were kept very busy.' One thing that always troubled men about women in signal boxes was, to quote Collie Knox: 'from where do they derive the strength to work the hand levers?' 'Yes the levers were heavy,' Doreen says 'but it's more of a knack. Once you have it, it's easy! First you release it, then you pull. It really wasn't a problem.' Neither was studying for the railway signalling exam by correspondence course. Doreen was very proud of passing. 'It was a good bit harder than the colour-blindness test,' she says laughingly, 'when you had to identify the colour of different coloured wools. Mind you, when I did it, the wools were so old and had been used so many times, they were nearly all one colour, grubby grey!' When nervous exhaustion took Doreen off signal work she was devastated. On doctor's order she could

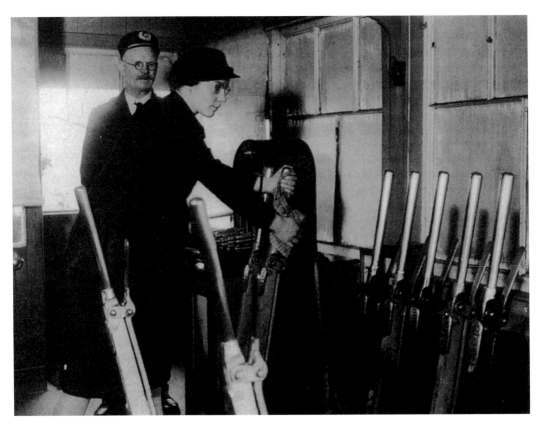

Mrs Mary Lewis's (*née* Jewell) father was a signalman on the main Paddington-Bristol line. Mary had already worked as a porter at Salford station for twenty months when he recommended her to the district inspector for signal work. Here she is at Pensford box under the watchful eye of Station Master Smewin, who was 'a no-nonsense man who liked everything to be just right', says Mary. 'It was good to be busy and organised as you could feel quite isolated in a box, especially during the blackouts.' After having received the air-raid telephone warnings, Mary had to turn the paraffin lamps down to low and use a hand lamp for entering train times into the log.

not return, but spent the rest of the war years working in Savernake booking office. She stayed there until after her marriage in 1948.

It was not just young girls that were responding to the call for women to replace men, or attracted to the thought of working in signal boxes. Mrs Beatrice 'Trixie' Dalwood (*née* Bird) was a forty-year-old full-time mother of five boys and one girl, ranging in age from ten to twenty-something, when she saw an advertisement in her local station, Wookey, asking for women to work in its signal box. Wookey, on the Yatton side of Wells, on what was know as the Cheddar Valley line, running from Yatton to Witham, was a small station and box, but a busy little place. Generally speaking, pre-war branch lines were relatively quiet, but during the war a lot of freight was diverted off the mainlines on to them. Wookey was a place where the trains would stop and the crews would change footplates working either back down or up the line to their original station. There was also a little shunting yard for St Cuthbert's Paper Works who were the main employer in the area. Regular goods trains would deliver the pulp and others take away the finished paper products.

Pensford box worked in conjunction with Marsh Junction box in the Bristol direction and Bromley sidings box in the south. It had the first passing-loop out of Bristol. A token was used for the former section and a staff for the latter. Engine drivers could not proceed without exchanging these with Mary as seen here, Engines would normally be stopped to do this, but some drivers liked to keep up the momentum to tackle the gradient towards Bristol and so would do it 'on-the-run', not always successfully, then they would have to stop the train and walk back to an amused Mary, for the change-over.

Trixie had no previous railway connections, but decided that signalwoman was the job for her, much to the delight of her husband, who worked at the paper mill. She lived within a few minutes walking distance of the station where the signal box was right on the platform. It was very handy as it did not take long to 'pop home' and to see to things when needed. Trixie shared shifts with Vera Fisher, another local woman of around thirty-five years. They would turn around shifts starting early in the morning one week and the afternoon the next. They did not work nights as the box closed around 10.30 p.m. after the last train. Despite the men's objections to women's entry into the boxes, most signalwomen said that they were treated kindly, especially by their station masters. Trixie was very fortunate, Mr Williams, her Station Master, was sympathetic to the difficulties of bringing up a family and would often allow her to see the children off to school when she was on the morning shift. In those days he could have easily 'held the fort' as stations masters would have had a broad training, having done most jobs in the station on their way up the career ladder. Audrey, Trixie's daughter, then just eleven years old, can remember sitting in the box, watching her mother whilst waiting for her to finish work. 'Oh, how she loved

Signal boxes had to be kept 'ship-shape'. Everything had to be kept cleaned snd in its place. Here Mary is organising the single-line token instrument. She stayed in Pensford box for over six years until she received a letter from Mr Smewin stating: 'I regret it is now necessary to terminate your employment … your services will not be required after 27 November 1948'.

it. She was happy as a sand-boy in there,' remembers Audrey. 'She had no trouble with the men, all the drivers liked her.' Trixie worked in the box until the end of the war, then she went back to being a full-time housewife.

1   All details taken from NRP2/23A Chester Record Office.
2   *Morning Post*, May 1918.
3   NRP2/23 Cheshire Record office.

# CHAPTER 8

# OTHER DEPARTMENTS

## Stores

Whilst there is little paper trail to show that women were working in the workshops during the First World War, there is evidence to show that they were taken on in the stores departments in both Swindon and Wolverhampton. The stores department was a vast operation. The head office and main stores were at Swindon. Worcester was the next in significance, certainly in terms of employees, but there were also large establishments at Wolverhampton, Reading, Didcot, Barry Docks and Barry, Cardiff and Bridgewater. The GWR believed in keeping things 'in-house' so stores was a vast enterprise covering everything from individual tools for the workmen to timber used in the making of carriages, material for making the Company's towels, dusters, uniforms, clogs, and, on occasions of a practical joke, even buckets of steam!

Application letters, GWR forms, and letters of reference, whether straight from school or previous employer, as well as GWR's medical forms, give fascinating insights into the context of the times. Take the details of Beatrice Louisa Davis, born May 1890 and residing in Morrison Street, Swindon. During the First World War she applied for a job as an issuer at Swindon General Stores. The GWR sent their standard letter dated 10 April 1917, to her previous employer, Mrs Barrett of Overy Manor, Dorchester, stating: 'I will be much obliged if you will reply to the inquiries given below, returning this form to me at your earliest convenience'. It is initialled WBC for H. Dean. The form does not allow for much detail in response to its specific questions, so answers are brief:

| | |
|---|---|
| In what capacity have you employed the person named above? | *Laundry Maid.* |
| How long was he in your employee? | *About nine months.* |
| When did he leave? | *March.* |
| Why did he leave? | *On account of sciatica.* |
| What did you pay him? | *22s per week.* |
| What are his qualifications as a Workman? | |
| Is he sober, honest and industrious? | *Mrs Davis is quite honest and sober.* |
| What is your opinion of his general character? | *Reliable.* |
| Date : 11 April 1917 | [Signed] *J C Barrett.* |

'Stores' was like Aladdin's cave being full of everything needed for the manufacture and maintenance of locomotives and rolling stock, as well as the running of the Company's 'other parts' including hotels, refreshment rooms and offices. The despatch department of the general stores, Swindon, was in the basement and gas mantles provided the main source of lighting.

In the section 'Why taken on' was entered: 'to replace Andrews (at 4/4 per day) who is joining the Army'. Beatrice started work on 10 April 1917 as a storeswoman in general stores, 'A' Floor, earning 3s per day. Eliza Hannah Coxon, born May 1879, of 25 Hughes Street, Swindon, had worked for four years as a parish nurse at Norbury Rectory, Nr Ashbourne, Derbyshire, earning between £35 and £45 per year. Her reference said she was a reliable, conscientious, clean and capable woman. She started the same day as Beatrice in the goods department. The reason for her employment was: 'To assist Watts in the Goods Shed'. Both applications were approved by Miss Howe, countersigned by WBC and marked as 'temporary'.

When applying for posts with GWR, women would play on their connections with the Company, either through relatives who worked there, i.e. fathers, brothers or uncles, or on the fact that they or their mother were widowed, or both. A letter dated 11 April 1917, from Constance Ada Truman, of 124 Morrison Street, Swindon, does just this. Constance wrote:

> Dear Sir
>
> I am writing to ask you if you have a vacancy for a young person. My age is eighteen years, and I have been working at Chandlers in Old Town but I had to leave on account of catching a chill. I am anxious to get some work to do so that I can help my mother, as my father was killed in the war and left Mother a widow with twelve children, and there are only two boys

at work, both of them in the boiler shop in the factory. I should be very pleased to receive an answer if you have a vacancy as a young friend told me you were wanting young girls.
I remain, yours respectfully,
C. Truman.

Constance had been employed at Chandlers Bros., as a showroom duster. Happily for the family, she was taken on by the GWR on 4 June 1917 as a packer in 'traffic', in place of a man called to the Colours, at the usual 3s per day. This was an immense increase over her last wage which had been 7s per week and would, undoubtedly, have been an enormous help to her mother. Another woman, a Mrs L. Norton, wrote:

> If you have a vacancy in your department as an issuer, I should be glad of your consideration. My late husband worked as a painter in the Carriage Department, under Messrs. Broome & Simms, for eleven years. He responded to the call … and was, unfortunately, killed in France last summer. I am twenty-eight years of age and anxious to get employment as my pension is insufficient to keep me. My father-in-law worked as a coach painter for the Company about forty-five years and is still employed by Mr Broome.

It was not just young girls seeking employment, but also older women with family responsibilities. Mrs M.J. Moulden of Highworth, was forty-eight at the time of her application in April 1917. Her husband had been killed in France and she needed to work.[1] She wrote:

> I was up to the Labour Exchange, but the Lady Clerk told me I was past the age, but I am able to do a days work with other women but they don't give you a chance, the Country and King has had our best and now they don't trouble about us that is left to battle with the world.

Mrs Moulden was taken on in the general stores 'A' Floor as storeswoman at 3s per day to temporarily replace Andrews (at 4s 4d per day) who was joining the Army.

Applications of women taken on in the Wolverhampton stores make interesting reading in that they show women are moving from different areas of employment, for reasons sometimes war connected, due to wages or perhaps because they did not like the job. Edith Parkins, born 1894, of West Street, Wolverhampton, had started work in 1912 in the factory of Messrs Manders Brothers, on a can-making machine. On a piecework wage she earned on average 18s a week. On applying to work for the GWR it was revealed Edith stayed for 'four years, eight months' in her previous employment. Answering the question 'was she sober, honest and industrious?' Manders Brothers wrote: 'As far as we know'. The reason given for her leaving there 'was to work on munitions'. She left there in February 1917. Her record shows that her next job started sometime in March and lasted about a month. She was employed as a trucker in the bond department of the works at Bushbury. Here she earned £1 per week. Their reason given for her leaving here is 'not satisfied with wages', however an attached handwritten note by Mr A.W. Cottell, the storekeeper, explains: 'Miss Parkins was ordered to load and unload trucks and this was the principle reason why she left.' Responding to the enquiry about 'general character', Mr Maurice Jones wrote: 'not here long enough to enable me to form a proper opinion'. Despite this, she was taken on, on 7 April 1917 as a packer in 'B' stores. Perhaps the fact that her father was a signalman with the GWR helped. Florence A. Whittall and Alice Crook, are interesting examples because, although they were just moving within the GWR, a completed reference form was still required. Mr J.A. Robinson, the divisional superintendent's office supplies the information for both women. They had both started in January 1916 as carriage cleaners in the carriage department, Victoria Basin, at 4½d per hour plus war bonus. Both are then transferred to 'A1' stores in April 1917, at 3s per day. Surprisingly, both were employed 'in place of G Chandler – on Military service'. Mr Chandler must have had a very demanding job as it required two women to replace him or perhaps it was just part of what had become accepted thinking in regard to the ratio of women needed to replace trained men as defined by Mr F.W. West, a goods superintendent of the SECR. Mr West had laid the foundation for this thinking when he told the *Daily Telegraph* in August 1915 that 'three untrained girls could undertake two trained men's duties'.

Looking at these applications it is interesting to note that even at this stage, three years into the war and after years of employing female workers, the GWR have not changed their forms to accommodate women applicants. The forms still denote 'he'. On some, such as for Miss Edith

---

**G.W.R. STORES DEPARTMENT,** WOLVERHAMPTON Station 3

**APPLICATION FOR EMPLOYMENT.** (23s)

500—A 18–5–13.

April 28th. 191 7.

| | | |
|---|---|---|
| 1 | Name in full | Alice Crook. |
| 2 | Address | 3 Dunstall St., Wolverhampton. |
| 3 | Height of Applicant, without boots | 5 feet 3 inches. |
| | | *Verified by Certificate* _____ 191__ |
| 4 | Date of Birth | August 16th, 1889. |
| 5 | State whether previously employed under G.W.R. in any Department | Yes. |
| | If so; where, and in what capacity | Carriage Dept., Victoria Basin. Carriage Cleaner. |
| | Between what dates | Jan.5th,16 to April 28th,17. |
| | Cause of leaving | – |
| 6 | In the case of youths, state if the father is in G.W.R. Co.'s service, and if so, give his name, occupation, and Station.. | – |
| 7 | State if enrolled in Militia, Army Reserve, or Navy Reserve | – |
| 8 | Reference for character†: Name and Business | J. A. Robinson, Esq., Divisional Superintendent |
| | † Reference must always be made to the last employer with whom the applicant has worked for three months or upwards if possible; in exceptional cases, where the previous employer cannot be referred to, the name and address of some other person must be given, the relation between the person to whom reference is made and the applicant must be stated, and also the reason why reference cannot be made to a previous employer. Address | Stafford Road, Wolverhampton. |
| | Applicant's occupation and Wages.. | Carriage Cleaner – 4½d per hour plus war bonus. |
| | How long in employ | From 5/1/16 to 28/4/17. |
| | Date and cause of leaving | 28/4/17.Transferred to Stores Dept. |
| | Signature of applicant for employment | A. Crook |

N.B.—Any wilful mis-statement in the information given above will render the applicant liable to dismissal from the Company's Service.

| | | |
|---|---|---|
| 9 | Date of starting work | April 30th, 1917. |
| 10 | Proposed Employment–Storehouse | "A1" Stores. |
| | Occupation | Storeswoman. |
| | Proposed Wages | 3/- per day. |
| | Why taken on* | Temporary. In place of G. Chandler, On Military service. |
| | * If in place of any other workman, the name and rate of wages of the workman leaving to be stated. | |

Signature of Storekeeper _____

Signature of Superintendent _____

---

Official forms can provide a lot of information regarding Company policy and practice. Here we can see that the GWR operated a height requirement policy for prospective male employees, as well as wanting to know the occupation of the applicant's father and about any previous relationship to the GWR. The latter was always helpful towards one's own application and many women used it to further their cause.

Parkin, of April 1917, they have taken the trouble to add an 's' in front of he to make it 'she', and crossed out 'him' and written in 'her', but for most others they simply did not bother. The GWR's application form required name; address; height 'without boots'; date of birth, whether employed previously in any GWR department and if so, when, where and reason for leaving; whether their father is employed with GWR and if so his name, occupation and station; whether one has served in the militia; the name and address of a character reference; the applicants previous occupation and wage; length of previous employment and reason for leaving. There is no request to know whether married or single, as these forms were designed with only men in mind and men would be expected to work whether they were married or not. By the middle years of the war the Company had instigated a new medical form for women, owing to the fact that much of the information required of the men was inapplicable, or singularly inappropriate to expect young girls or married women to provide. On the men's form there was the usual requirement for name, address, post applied for and date of birth. As GWR operated a minimum height expectation of 5ft 4in or, but if on the passenger side, 5ft 6in it was necessary for men to register their height. It was also required to know their weight and an 'ideal' weight was given for between these two heights: not less than 140lb. In the 'measurement of chest' section – it was required that a measurement be taken 'under arm-pits and over nipples,' and also 'shape of same', It also required the measurement of the chest at rest and at deep inspiration. In respect of 'head and neck' they wanted to know about nasal polypus and 'absess of glands'. The latter could be caused by tuberculosis, a virulent problem then. They also required examination of the mouth and throat looking at enlarged tonsils, very defective teeth and defect in speech. Also the chest and lungs were examined to check if there was flattening from Pleurisy or a curved spine as well as the 'character of the sounds of the heart'. Under 'abdomen' came the requirement for details on scars of old syphilis, enlarged testis or venereal disease. Such sexual conditions had, for many long years, been a continuing problem amongst the population, no matter which class they belonged to. It was not, therefore, out of the ordinary for the GWR to request this information of men, but, bearing in mind the conservative and patriarchal nature of the GWR, prudish in their outlook and delicate in their thinking in respect of 'the fair sex', they would, undoubtedly, have found using these forms with women more than a little distasteful.

The GWR had instigated some forms for women in respect of clerical work and so had rolled out the use of these for other 'temporary' females.

The 'Medical Examination of Candidate for Employment on the Female Labour Staff' form required the usual information in respect of name, address, grade and department applied for and age. Thereafter there was an abbreviated and modified version of the male form.

Number 10, however, differs significantly from the men's. It asks: 'Has candidate ever been an inmate of a lunatic asylum or suffered from any mental affliction?' At this time women were much more likely to have been consigned to an asylum or be considered to be suffering from a mental condition than men, as it was believed that being unstable or temperamental, i.e. 'mental', was inherent in their nature. Lunatic asylums were also used to 'contain' women for all sorts of reasons, such as getting pregnant before marriage or other 'deviant' behaviour, therefore this question would have been perceived as being relevant for the women but not the men, and the questions regarding venereal disease were not thought applicable to the women, despite the fact that women suffered the consequences of infected men. Luckily for Rose Bray, aged twenty-five, of Evans Street, Wolverhampton, the examining surgeon was able to answer 'normal' to all the necessary questions and 'no' to No.10, and pass her as being 'in good health, of sound constitution and fit for Railway Service'. Rose started work as a storeswoman in 'A2' stores, Wolverhampton, in August 1923 earning 3s 7d per day plus 2s 6d per day bonus. Having, presumably, learned from the experience the first time around, the GWR got its act together more quickly for the Second World War female

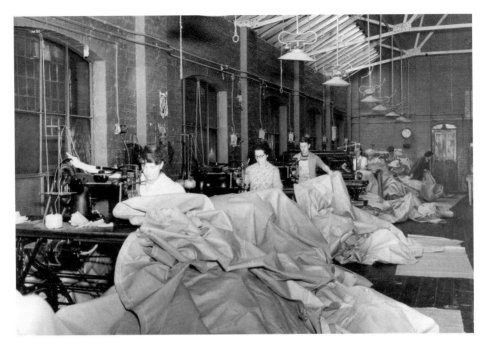

*Above and below:* Women's traditional skills were put to use in unexpected places – in the sewing room of the GWR's sheet shops, such as that at Worcester. An article in the *Magazine* in 1932 explains how the women sewed the undressed canvas into sheets and also worked on the grommeting machine, inserting and sewing the rings at a speed of up to eighty per hour. During the Second World War more women were taken on to help repair the tarpaulins. 'Sewing is a woman's sphere,' writes the *Magazine* in 1943, 'yet the work entailed in repairing these tarpaulins, many of them weighing nearly 1cwt each, is very heavy and exacting, but these women are performing their various wartime tasks very ably.'

recruitment and when Mrs Vera Nancy Watson applies for a post her details are entered on form 38 G: 'Application for Employment in Replacement of Staff, Serving With HM Forces (Terminable by One Week's Notice)'. The form has changed a great deal in respect of details required. Gone is the requirement to know whether the father was previously in the Militia and whether he works only for the company, now they want to know for whom he works, no matter which company. Gone is the requirement to know height without boots and gone is the need to know previous wage.

The stores department offered a number of opportunities to women workers in both its shops and its offices. The 1922 Census of Staff for the Stores Department shows a staff return of sixty-five office females, three of whom are junior girl clerks. The Census of 1929 shows there are ninety-nine women and two girl clerks, thirteen women and four juniors in 'shops' and three 'other' adult women in the stores department making a total of 115 female staff.[2] These figures increase significantly during the Second World War. The 1942 Stores' Census shows a return of twenty-eight office girls and 154 adult female clerks. In 1947, the last GWR Census for the Stores Department, there forty-six juniors and 123 female adult clerks.

## Traffic Department

### Charwomen

Cleaning was seen as women's natural role. If you were a working-class woman, cleaning was an occupation that you were destined for from birth. Whether you did it unpaid in your own home for your family or paid in other people's homes, it shaped a major part of your life. During the nineteenth and early twentieth century, cleaning was one of the few paid occupations open to working-class women and huge numbers of women were absorbed into domestic service either as live-ins or dailies. Women's early entry into the railway world as a paid employee (women had already entered the railway world as shareholders) was in this domestic capacity under the grade of charwoman or cleaner.

The Staff Registers of the London and North Western and Great Western Joint Railway, record a number of women in such positions and one can chart the line of women employed at Chester over a number of years. In 1854 M. Diamond, aged thirty-five years, entered the Company's service earning 8s 3d. In 1877 she received a pay rise up to 11s and in February 1878, aged fifty-eight, she resigned. She was replaced in February by I. Eden who started on the 11s rate. For reasons not recorded she left in April 1878. Next came Mrs Vaughan who started in July 1878 at the same rate. Mrs Vaughan was dismissed for insubordination in August 1887. Another interesting entry is that of Mrs Corbett who replaced a Mrs Coates at Craven Arms. Mrs Coates had started in 1869 on 4s per week as a cleaner and left in March 1881 incapacitated by illness. Mrs Corbett, however, is identified by the more elevated title of office cleaner. She started in April 1881 at 6s, resigned in December 1884 and started again in April 1888 at 7s. Station refreshment rooms and railway hotels were other places where women would have been taken on in this capacity. A women's room attendant or waiting room attendant of which there were several recorded, was really a cleaner by another name, but with more specialised duties, and with a slightly higher wage scale. A Census of Staff for 1914 shows that the largest number of women then employed on the passenger side was charwomen of which there were 138 earning from 2s per week up to a surprising 27s 3d.

### Carriage Cleaners

Society regarded cleaning as a woman's job, but not on trains. Yes in their hotels and refreshment rooms. Yes in the ladies waiting rooms and offices. Not, however, in the engine sheds. Engine cleaning and carriage cleaning were men's jobs. Whilst one can, perhaps, understand the thinking

During the First World War it was widely believed that women of a large and robust physique were most suitable for carriage cleaning. Obviously Mrs Lily Mary Walter (*née* Greenwood) was not, yet she, and Mrs Fluck, Diana Dors's mother, proved perfectly capable of cleaning railway carriages at Swindon during this period.

Despite huge numbers of women having always been employed as cleaners in domestic service as well as railway offices, refreshment rooms, hotels and waiting rooms, these female cleaners are something of a curiosity because they are employed as carriage cleaners, something rarely done by women before the First World War. Carriage cleaning, inside and out, was a physically demanding job and thought too difficult for women to perform.

on engines, which were large, difficult to climb over in long skirts and viewed as potentially dangerous machines, why not carriages? In the infancy of the railways, carriages were large and cumbersome things. It would have been thought inappropriate to have women climbing up and over them to clean the outsides, but why not the insides? Pratt records that a few railway companies had employed a few women – who had 'proved their usefulness' – as cleaners but it was not until the First World War that any numbers of significance were taken on. It is incredibly ironical that it took an event of world-shattering proportions for railway men, unions and companies to allow women to perform what was always considered their role to do and clean carriages, and, heaven forbid, engines.

During the First World War the NUR fought hard to protect their members' jobs and keep women out of cleaning. *The Chronicle & Cheshire, North Wales Advertiser* reported under the heading 'Shortage of Labour on the Lines' that:

> The NUR are asking that the companies should meet the position (the shortage of staff) by promoting lower grades and make good the shortage in the lower grades by calling in casual labour … suitable casual labour is not to be found – save by employing women as cleaners, a course to which the men are opposed...

A further course was to bring in even younger boys, aged fourteen, and straight from school, but this did not prove very satisfactory and so the railway companies had little choice but to take 'the revolutionary step' and take on women.

Edwin Pratt expressed society's view when he wrote: 'carriage cleaning was an occupation well-suited to those belonging to the working classes'. Goods superintendent, Mr F.W. West elaborated further saying that 'women better qualified by physique than education', should be suitably engaged. *The Railway Gazette* of August 1915 agrees, saying: 'they have shown a natural aptitude for carriage cleaning', however, forever championing the railwaymen's cause, it goes on to say that though women's work in this respect is satisfactory: 'even here it is questionable whether the work formerly performed by a given number of men can be covered by the same number of women; six females to five males has been reckoned a fair comparison'. Most agreed that the women, although held to be slower than the men, were also held to be more thorough and they had proved 'eminently satisfactory' capturing 'the sympathies of the railway traveller'.

The GWR took on female carriage cleaners in sheds up and down the line and over the war period their magazine shows several such pictures. For example, a crowd of forty-nine women and three men at Old Oak Common in 1915; a handful of women surrounding one lone male, who is just about to depart to the Colours at Newton Abbott in 1916; and seventeen women very smartly kitted out in uniform at Birkenhead in 1919. Records show that Florence A. Whittal and Allice Crook were taken on at Wolverhampton in 1916. Their wage was 4½d per hour plus war bonus. By the end of the war the GWR employed 594 women and 153 men carriage cleaners. Something of a major turn-around. By the 1930s, however, things were changing back again. *The Railway Year Book* shows that in 1931 there were 742 female carriage cleaners employed on all the railways and by 1934/35 only 456.

## Locomotive sheds

### *Good Depots*

In the First World War there had been a general disbelief about the ability of women to be porters, let alone work in the Company's goods sheds, yet by 1918 the GWR had employed 616 female goods porters.

*Above:* Cleaning the smokebox: Mrs Mercy Whelan hated doing this job. 'I hated going in there,' she said. 'It was filthy!' These clean women must be at the beginning of their shift!

*Opposite above:* Locomotive-shed labouring was one of the dirtiest, hardest and most unpleasant jobs on the railways. Despite initial reservations regarding women's physical stamina and capabilities they were eventually taken on to do such heavy manual jobs. The women's mantra for that time – 'It was the war, we just got on with it' – speaks volumes regarding their whole-hearted commitment to helping the war effort.

*Opposite below:* Engine cleaner had always been the first rung on the traditional ladder to becoming an engine driver, the job of all jobs on the railways. The drivers, to use the words of Mr Roy Newton were 'Gods' and their deputies, the firemen 'Saints'. Roy says, 'Engine cleaning was not a job for the faint hearted.' The first thing was to collect the cotton waste and cleaning oil. Next – one quickly learnt – was to feel through the waste checking for pieces of swarfe, i.e. metal bits, that, if not taken out, could rip your fingers very badly. With this done, the waste was divided into useful parts and the cleaner then soaked one part in the cleaning oil. Next, the excess was squeezed out and cleaning began. The exterior of the whole locomotive had to be cleaned from the very top, down to the last wheel rim. Roy remembers that 'there were three female cleaners at Llantrisant who were not allowed to go above footplate height – the age of equality had not yet arrived. Their cleaning was from that level down, including the horrible wheels not a pleasant job for male hands much less so for ladies'. (All photographs courtesy of the University of Leicester)

Barrowing large and awkward cases and parcels over cobbles is never easy. You had to be tough and determined. The women, none the less, seem to have the measure of the job at Bristol goods station in 1941. Over 250 were employed there during the war. (Photograph courtesy of the University of Leicester)

During the Second World War a new attitude to female porters began to prevail. Whilst it still held that goods porterage was a hard, physical job, deemed beyond women's physical capabilities without special concessions, propaganda press articles were now proclaiming that any woman, with the right attitude, could, and should, do it and bring up a family at the same time:

Mother of 15 Is Now A Porter:
'Am I tired when I finish work? Not a bit of it', says Mrs. Russell. 'I start at eight in the morning and finish at five o'clock. When I get home there is time to do a good wash'.
(*Daily Herald* February 1941)

In the *Magazine* a whole article under the heading 'Women Porters "Go To It" on the GWR' is devoted to the fact that there are now over 500 women employed in the Company's larger freight depots alone. It tells us that an advertisement for women porters placed in a Bristol local paper brought a 'steady stream of applicants'. Over 250 were employed there. It would seem that these women had the 'stoutest of hearts' as they were undeterred by the 'vastness of Temple Meads goods station [at this time the World's largest covered goods station]

There is a striking contrast between the smiling young women and the older men (many former retirees re-engaged for war work) in this remarkable photograph of Paddington goods shed during the Cornish broccoli season. Once numerous special trains were run to accommodate this annual traffic, which is now completely lost to the railways. No concessions are made for the female porters and their trolleys are fully laden. (Photograph courtesy of the University of Leicester)

and the many long trolley runs between wagon and lorry'. 'Suitably attired' they took their place in the gangs and learnt a variety of methods of transporting the goods, only 'occasionally needing a helping hand when the wheel of a heavily laden trolley stuck in a rut'. The Company gives them a pat on the back by stating: 'they are tackling their job with zeal and enthusiasm', alongside a veiled implication that should things go awry it would be the women's fault: 'we have every confidence that they will not let the Company down during the momentous times ahead'.

1   A reference written for her by her husband's employer, the Head Master at Highworth Council School states this – information form STEAM Museum, Swindon.
2   Census of Staff 1929. David Hyde Collection.
3   Census of Staff 1914. David Hyde Collection

130

*Above:* Miss Irene Bannister of Worcester aged twenty-two, was the first woman to qualify as a telephone and communications maintainer on the GWR. She was the first woman on the GWR and probably in the country to take up an appointment as a linesman's assistant, although technically she was doing the linesman's work as she was fault-finding. Miss Nellie Cox, assisting on the left, was following in Irene's footsteps. Here they are seen checking the integrity of an electrical installation using an anometer to check the voltage. Irene's ability to read blue prints was described as 'amazing'.

*Opposite above:* In the days before continuously welded rail and automated track machines scenes such as this were commonplace on the railways. This platelayers gang is the usual wartime mix of older men and young women. They are carrying out routine work of cleaning and packing the sleepers and levelling up the track joints to ensure a smooth and safe ride for the passengers.

*Opposite below:* An all-female gang of platelayers at Bristol West Depot, in March 1943, get on with the job as shunting operations continue unabated in the background. Keith Steele remembers a Mrs Mills who worked as a platelayer in a gang working out from West Bromwich signal box. With a scraper in one hand and an oil feed in the other she would first scrape the slides to remove any dirt, then oil them, then shout to the signalmen to reverse the points and then repeat the cleaning process. This done, she would shout again and request he returned the points to normal. Mrs Mills also worked on measured shovel packing, opening out beds (this requires removing ballast between two sleepers), or walking the length of the track with a key hammer knocking in any wooden keys that had fallen out. Other times she would act as a 'lookout' for the rest of the gang working on the track. (All photographs courtesy of the University of Leicester)

*Above:* Mary Evelyn Woodfield is proud to have been a real linesman's assistant. She had to wait for another female to be assigned to the same work before she could start, so she would not be on her own with the men! Mary remembers: 'My job was to help the-man-in-charge, either Dan Bevan or his mate Harry Dart. He would find the faults when the signals failed to function. I would clean away any debris, i.e. ballast stones, clogged up earth or any build up of dirt and then oil around the wheels that were wired to the signals. My tools for the job were one small scraper, one hand brush and one oil can, all of which were provided. Sometimes we had to clean out the dirty, scruffy cabin and light the fire. There was a lot of walking between boxes, but we always got a warm welcome and cuppa from the signalmen and thanks for "a clean job done". They remarked that since we (the women) had been on the job there were fewer problems because the cleaning was done better. There were three boxes in the yard at Severn Tunnel Junction. It was a very busy, noisy and dirty place. Most of the men were saucy but I gave as good as I got while still keeping my dignity, but they were all respectful, maybe because they knew my Dad who was on the GWR. No one resented us, we were very much a novelty as there hadn't been any women in the yard before.' Mary's only regret was that she did not get any training to take on more responsibility. 'They would say, "never you mind, you just stay in the hut till we sort it out"; it made me a bit cross.'

*Opposite above:* These girls outside a typical corrugated iron lampman's hut are cleaning and priming the burners which were used in signal lamps. The long wooden handle in the foreground was used to carry the lamps. (Photograph courtesy of the University of Leicester)

*Opposite below:* The lamplady places the prepared lamp interiors in the signal lamp on a bracket signal. Since some signals could be over 30ft in height, a strong head for heights was a prerequisite for this vitally important job. (Photograph courtesy of the University of Leicester)

# CHAPTER 9

# DISTINCTIVE WOMEN

Whilst many of the women who worked for the GWR were 'distinctive' in that they carved new territories for women workers or challenged established conventions, some stand out for special attention. In different ways their stories, the way they are treated, reported or reviewed at the time, highlight the place of women in society, in the workplace and on the railways. Their individual stories indirectly show us the limitations placed on women in general at those times. They also give us insight into the changing relationship of women and the GWR. Trying to find the voice of these women to tell their own stories is difficult, if not impossible, because even when they do 'speak' it is usually to tell us about the company, such as with Miss Shirtliff, and not about themselves; most times they do not speak at all. Sometimes they are distinctive because of the rarity of what they did, as with Elsie Winterton and the Dening sisters, but at other times it is because of outstanding acts performed in the line of duty, like May Owen. In every other sense these are ordinary women living everyday lives, but with the status that came from working for the GWR.

## The Dening Sisters

When Freda Effie Dening died, aged ninety-seven in 1995 the *Evening Advertiser* announced her passing with the headline 'Death of a Pioneer'. Freda was an outstanding woman for her time, as was her sister Irene. They had followed their brother Henry into Swindon Works and they then followed him with winning the prestigious Brunel Medal, Freda in 1921 and Irene in 1922.

The Brunel Medal was endowed by Lord Winterstoke, a GWR director. It was an impressive medal in many respects. It was crafted in silver in the original GWR die-stamp which was gifted by the Company to the railway department of the London School of Economics. A splendid head of Brunel graces the front and on the back there is an engraving of the Royal Albert Bridge which spans the river Tamar, built by Brunel at Saltash in 1859. The medal was instituted in 1907/08 and was first won by a GWR employee, Mr W.G. Chapman of the general manager's office and two other non-GWR students. Out of a total of 176 medals, seventy-six have been won by members of the GWR staff. It was a much coveted medal, but like many of Brunel's own achievements, it took years of hard work, determination and application to achieve. The *Magazine* explains:

*Above, left and right:* Miss Freda Effie Dening and her sister Irene Alice Dening, known to her work colleagues as 'Den', were two of only a handful of women to achieve the coveted Brunel Medal in 1921 and 1922 respectively. They both had long and satisfying careers with the GWR.

> The Brunel Medal is awarded to students in the railway department of the London School of Economics who, in not more than four years, have obtained three first class passes in examinations held in connection with courses approved for the purpose.

In 1912 when Freda was just fourteen, she 'entered the service of the GWR', starting in the statistical section of the engineer's office at Marlow House, which was situated behind Swindon Junction station. She was among the first clerical girls to be employed at Swindon Works. It was a time when, as the *Evening Advertiser* put it, 'few women got on to the career ladder', yet just nine years later Freda became the first woman of any railway company to receive the special honour of the Brunel Medal, closely followed by Irene. Freda had wanted to get on and studied shorthand and typing at Swindon College. She became a shorthand typist in the offices, probably during the First World War. She was, however, a bold spirit and an obviously intellectually able young woman so in 1918 she took the opportunity to study accounting and business methods, the law of carriage by railway, the basis of railway rates and charges, and the principal factors in railway operating for the next three years, all after putting in a full day's work. For Freda it was worth it; not only did she pass, she achieved three first-class certificates and so, on 5 August 1921, Freda received a letter from the secretary of the London School of Economics and Political Science telling her:

I am desired by the Director to inform you that you have been awarded the Brunel Silver Medal. Please accept my heartfelt congratulations on your success. The medal will be sent to you in the course of a few weeks, when it has been received from the makers.

Yours very truly,

J. Mair

Secretary

How thrilled she must have been to prove, as her niece, Dr Barbara Carter says, 'that if her brother could do it, then she could do it too!' Irene must have been overjoyed to complete the trio just a year later. The *Magazine* announced in July 1922 'three members in one family is probably a unique achievement' and 'heartily congratulated the recipients upon their successes' urging other staff with several family members in the service to take heed and follow suit.

In 1921 Freda was transferred to the personal staff of the CME. All around her young women were leaving the railway service to get married, but Freda stayed, preferring her freedom, her work and her travel. For a handful of women who remained single, such as Freda and Irene, their work at the GWR offered not only a lifelong career and a satisfying work experience but was also a means to financial independence and a liberation and freedom from local confines

Christmas decorations in the Stores Department office, Swindon Works. Irene Denning – third row back, seated first left – was secretary to the stores superintendent when this photograph was taken. She had a very senior and important position for a woman, although, obviously, it came with few trimmings and she sat with the others at the traditional long desks. Many women spoke of the offices 'feeling like a schoolroom', seeing everyone sat in these regimented rows of desks with all eyes front – one can easily see why they felt that way.

offering as it did opportunities for travel far and wide on both free and subsidised tickets. This was a much valued bonus and one that Freda was reluctant to give up. The GWR also offered a social network through its many varied clubs and associations.

In 1927 Freda moved into the position where she was to spend her last twenty-five years, on the staff of the Locomotive Works' manager, where she was responsible for the organisation and supervision of the Locomotive Works typists' office. It was a senior position for a woman and there were non higher. Such a supervisory post for a female clerk was held in high regard within the railway offices, but Freda had reached her glass ceiling. Despite all their hard work and application and although they both studied accountancy and law, this knowledge was not put to use by GWR. It was within their 'female office skills' of shorthand and typing that Freda and Irene were mainly occupied. However, as Freda told a reporter from the *Swindon Advertiser*: 'I really loved my job and it opened many doors to opportunity that my sister and I would not of otherwise had. There were very few women in the railways in those days and it was a fascinating place to be.'

Whilst she chose not to marry, Freda could not entirely throw off the domestic responsibilities required of women and retired early to look after her failing parents. Knowing her passion for travel to Scotland, Ireland and even Europe, her colleagues presented her with a leather handbag and suitcase.

Irene Dening had a hard act to follow when she went into Swindon Works in 1914 but she was more than capable of doing so. Irene, whilst equally capable was 'more of a laugh', according to her niece, Barbara. 'She was more relaxed with people,' so much so that she had a nickname 'Den'. You can tell that she was held in high regard by the fact that at her retirement, three stores superintendents came along to her farewell ceremony, one, Mr H.R. Webb, reappearing from retirement himself. Unlike many women who worked inside Swindon Works' offices, Irene had close working contact with men and very senior 'big bosses'. She worked in the stores department and, over the years, in a secretarial capacity to four stores superintendents. It was a position of trust as well as responsibility. At the end of a nearly forty-five-year career on the railways, Irene retired in 1960. She had served under six stores superintendents or rather, to quote Mr R.B. Hoff, chief supplies officer of the BTC, 'they had all served under Den'.[1]

## Miss Elsie Winterton

Miss Elsie Louisa Winterton was an unusual woman, if not something of a rarity, especially for her time and especially in the masculine world of railways. Elsie had the distinction of not only being a draughtswoman in the signal engineer's office at Reading, but also of being the first woman to become an Associate Member, or to use the words as quoted in the *GWR Magazine*, the first '*Lady* Associate Member', of the Institute of Railway Signal Engineers.

Born in 1897 the sixth daughter and third youngest of nine children, in Newtown, Reading, Elsie, like her seven sisters (her brother had died in infancy), left school at fourteen without any formal qualifications. However, she, and her two younger sisters, Ella May (b.1900) and Doris 'Dorrie' Mabel (b.1904) had 'something about them' and managed to pass the entrance test and be taken on by the GWR. Elsie started at Reading in 1915, aged eighteen and Ella joined in 1916 when she was sixteen. Dorrie joined the GWR later in 1929 but worked up the line at Paddington station. Later their niece Jean also joined the Company working in the payroll offices of the catering department. Both Elsie and Ella worked their way up to become draughtswomen, whilst Doris became a tracer, both good jobs for men let alone for young women. Although a war-entry employee Elsie managed to be taken on or transferred to permanent staff so she was

'Woman in a Man's World' – England's first *Lady* Associate Member of the Institute of Signalling Engineers in 1923 at their summer meeting in Brussels. Elsie Winterton achieved this distinction through her academic attainments at the age of twenty-six while working as a draughtswoman in the drawing office at Reading. An Associate Member then is equivalent to a full member now.

not laid off when the men returned. Ella, however, was a temporary substitute and had to leave in 1919. She rejoined later aged twenty-four and was then employed in 'a posh job' in the drawing office at Paddington. She worked in the parliamentary section dealing with Westminster. At that time the Company was buying up land and important plans had to be delivered to various offices for agreement or notification. Ella often travelled by taxi, at the Company's expense, to deliver these plans and said she was told 'if you can't get in, break a window and throw it in'. Ella remembered that 'at this time there was great competition on the railways but it was a time when people took pride in their work, whatever their grade. The GWR was tip-top then.'

Elsie Winterton obviously 'found herself' in her work. It opened up possibilities of discovering and fulfilling her potential, at least academically. Between 1915 and 1924 she attended evening classes at University College, Reading, and studied electricity and magnetism, applied mechanics, general physics, chemistry, mathematics and machine construction and drawing, passing many with distinction. She showed immense capability in this field and was awarded by the college the Owen Ridley Prize for machine construction in 1919–20 and achieved the Wells Prize for Science in 1921–22. Both monetary prizes were awarded to students attending evening classes who 'deserved most credit for their work'.

Reports of her election to the Institute in both the *GWR Magazine* and *The Railway Magazine* in September 1923 inform the reader that Miss Winterton, no mention of her first name in either, started work in the drawing office in March 1915 as a tracer and became a draughtswoman in 1917. They tell how her work involved 'making wiring diagrams of electric signal appliances in connection with track circuits, signal and point machines, etc'. A report in a local newspaper, however, announces: 'England has acknowledged its first woman signal engineer' and makes the comparison: 'she knows as much about physics, mathematics and electricity as the average girl knows about jazz and cream cakes', highlighting just how unusual this achievement was in the age of flappers and frivolity.

Minutes of the July General Meeting of the Signal Engineer's Institution record: 'there are seventeen additional members elected to the Institution, among these is the first lady member.' The Annual Report for 1923 makes specific mention of the event recording: 'Miss Winterton possesses technical qualifications which the Council considers fully entitles her to membership of the Institution.' Elsie received a Certificate of Associate Membership dated 18 July 1923 – an Associate Member then is equivalent to a Full Member today. Such is the impact that Elsie's membership made on the Institution that she is mentioned again in very friendly terms in the report of the Annual General Meeting. When proposing a vote of thanks to the retiring president, Mr R.J. Insell, GWR signal engineer at Reading, Mr C.H. Ellison stated:

> During this year there have been two honours conferred upon Mr Insell, [that] will undoubtedly have added to the pleasure of his year in office. The first was his election to signal engineer of the Great Western Railway.
>
> The second honour which has been conferred upon him, and [of which] I am sure that every member feels a pang of jealousy and disappointment that it should have fallen to Mr Insell's lot, was to introduce the first lady member of this Institution. I am very sorry she did not come two years ago when the pleasure would have been mine.

Elsie very much enjoyed her membership and the experiences it offered her. In the year of her admittance she attended the Summer Meeting held in Brussels. A photograph shows her as the only woman amongst some seventy distinguished-looking gentlemen. Later in the year she is identified as having attended the Institution's Annual Dinner in the Great Central Hotel, Marylebone. In subsequent years she attended the Summer Meeting in Southampton (1924), in Belgium (1925) and a summer convention in Holland (1929). She was enjoying the fruits of her hard work and appears to have been comfortable being the only woman amongst so many men. Perhaps she had become used to such a situation at work. A 1919 photograph of the staff of the signal and telegraph engineers' department shows eight young female staff and twenty-two male staff, and another of around 1922, shows just five female staff and around sixty-six males.

There is no evidence that Elsie's academic prowess and attainments earned her any special progress through the ranks in the drawing office or on to a position of higher responsibility. Once she had reached the position of draughtswoman she stayed there. When she left to get married in 1930, she was, she wrote: 'drawing the top wage of 70s per week as a draughtswoman'. However, Elsie and Ella took up all the opportunities that working for the GWR gave to them. They loved to go on their office outings, and both were members of the GWR ladies hockey team. Ella usually played in goal. Elsie was also very active with St John's Ambulance work and was the captain of the 1929 ladies team competing in the GWR Director's Challenge Shield. Elsie had a creative side and liked to do illuminated lettering for memorials and posters.

In 1930, aged twenty-seven, Elsie married Edward Deacon, who worked as a draughtsman in the same department and was also a member of the Institute. Her leaving was announced in the *GWR Magazine* and Mr G.H. Crook, assistant to the signal engineer, 'referred in appreciative terms [to] her capabilities at work'. Widowed nine years later, life was difficult and money tight. At the outbreak of war she was invited to return to work in her old office. Despite being in such a

The Winterton sisters Dorrie, Ella, and Elsie Winterton all worked for the GWR. Daisy (second from right) did not. What an attractive family they were!

respected job with a respected company, Elsie always struggled financially to keep family and home going, having to pay for childcare whilst she worked. In 1947, the last year of the GWR, she was 'put in charge of a pool of female tracers', a new innovation at that time. Elsie never remarried, but stayed on after Nationalisation remaining at the Reading office until she retired in 1962. Ironically, although she had originally been on the permanent staff, Elsie had broken her service and on her return she did not meet the age conditions to be taken into the newly introduced superannuation scheme. When she retired, therefore, at the age of sixty-five after thirty-seven years of employment on the railways, there was no pension. Ella and Doris on the other hand, had been taken on the scheme and both had good pensions. Eventually Elsie was awarded a small ex-gratia pension.

Elsie Deacon (*née* Winterton) came from an unremarkable background. Her family was ordinary, or, to use the words of her great niece Mrs Jacqueline Harbor, who, after researching the family history found 'they all appeared to be upright, honest citizens who were only born, got married (in some cases) and then died without leaving a mark on anything'. I would suggest however, that in one way this was a remarkable family. Railway employment was then an unlikely career path for any woman – let alone a woman who had no railway connections – yet this family produced four women who, with only the basic education of the time, joined a prestigious company, earned their way into respected positions, and made careers in railway employment, paving the way for other women to follow. Elsie Winterton undoubtedly left her mark. She will have been recorded in the annals at Reading University as a winner of two of their prestigious prizes. She will also have been recorded in the Institute of Railway Signalling Engineers, not merely as a 'lady' member, which is something of value in its own right, but with the distinction of being the first lady member. The institute itself is at present writing up an acknowledgement of all its 'firsts' and Elsie Winterton will be amongst them. That mark is indelible.

Miss Audrey Shirtliff a 'ground-breaker', being the first saleswoman on any British railway in 1936. The GWR were so proud!

## Miss Audrey Shirtliff

The 1930s may have been a time of depression for some of the traditional industries bringing great difficulties for many families of the men employed there, but it was also a time of development and growth in the emerging 'light' industries of consumer products such as radios, cars and vacuum cleaners and people in these regions enjoyed a new prosperity. This prosperity brought new opportunities for leisure, sports and travel. The 1930s saw an explosion in excursions or 'outings' and the railways were keen to capitalise on this market.

The 1930s was also the time when a new phenomenon, led by the GWR, hit the railways and the country: 'Saleswoman,' as proudly proclaimed in the *Magazine*. 'The first to act for a British Railway company.' This new position was such an innovation and novelty that it was interesting enough to make the national press. She was heralded as the 'Railway Saleswoman' by the *News Chronicle* and *Daily Herald* but 'woman canvasser' or 'outings advisor', by Sir Robert Horne, the chairman of the GWR, when he announced her appointment at the Company's Annual General Meeting in 1937. The reason Sir Robert gave for employing her in this somewhat high-profile position was, 'because nobody but a woman knows what women really want'.

Miss Audrey Shirtliff of Chelsea, described by the papers variously as: 'young, smiling, attractive, brunette' and, intriguingly, 'wise in the ways of her sex', took up her post in September 1936. She was an experienced traveller both in the United Kingdom and abroad, as well as an accomplished linguist. She had previously worked in the advertising department of the *News Chronicle*, so was competent in selling ideas and packages. Although appointed to the office of the superintendent of the line, her job would require her to: 'travel all over the Great Western system interviewing the secretaries of women's political and social organisations, women's clubs, girls schools and factories, offering them outings'.

This in itself is quite startling. At this time, when women went to work they normally went to one place where they were generally managed and overseen. They did not wander all over the country, unaccompanied and unsupervised. Whilst the country was used to travelling salesmen, a travelling saleswoman was a different kettle of fish. Miss Shirtliff was indeed a woman in a man's world. The only safety net for the men was that she was selling only to women in an area men would find hard to access. It is quite startling that the GWR, previously so conservative in their approach to women, were now, some fifty years after they had resisted taking them on, not only happy to promote her through the media, but actually leading the way in a new career for women which challenged the accepted norms of the day! Obviously once again it comes down to money, but not cost cutting this time. Miss Shirtliff's job was to create new streams of revenue, and to do so she, like the early station masters, had to go out and sell the Company's services to new clients.

It is intriguing to see that just one month later, on 19 November, a Mrs Betty Gardner of Swindon became the first woman to ever address the GWR Lecture and Debating Society at Paddington. More interestingly the title of her lecture was 'Women's Place in Business – Should it be Extended or Curtailed?' This historical event was reported in the Company's magazine. The writer of the article, presumably a gentleman, in all senses of the word, remarks in a gentlemanly manner: 'Her speech was not only thoughtful in content but was delivered in a most charming and vivacious manner and quite captured her audience.' He also notes that she was: 'too sweetly reasonable to be very controversial.' One of the points made by Mrs Gardner was that there were numerous callings for which women were particularly well equipped in the working world. She identifies these as nurses and schoolteachers (both traditionally accepted areas for women to work in), clerks (a well-established type of employment since the First World War) and, more surprisingly saleswomen. Was it, one wonders, the appointment of Miss Shirtliff that made her include this still rather radical occupation for women?

By the time she was interviewed by the *Daily Herald* in February 1937 Audrey Shirtliff already had several months' experience tucked under her belt. Her remarks give an insight into the realities of women's lives of that time. 'I discovered,' she told them, 'thousands of women in the west of England have never been to London but wanted to go. Women's parties ask me to help arrange a day in London, including a trip to Buckingham Palace … and the shops. You see, there's a tremendous lot of pleasure in looking in shop windows, even if you've no intention of buying anything.' It is interesting to note that when we get to hear women speaking for themselves we learn incidentally so much about women's lives in general.

Two years later, Miss Shirtliff found that it is very difficult to discover who is the right woman to contact in the hundreds of different guilds, sisterhoods, mothers' groups and political associations that women belong too. The best way she has found she writes in the *Magazine*, is to 'ask the vicar or minister' or 'the village general shop – they know everything'.

Audrey's post would nowadays be called event management. It would require a lot of different skills – people skills, organisational skills, promotional skills, selling and administration skills, all rolled into one. She herself described it as 'selling travel', an 'altogether enthralling job'. The GWR described it as 'the promotion of outings and excursions', and 'advising in regards to itineraries, sight-seeing, amusements and catering, etc.' For Audrey that would have involved arranging road, steamer or air travel in conjunction with rail journeys, fixing meals or booking theatre – or any other – tickets required. In fact, almost anything that would get the women on to the GWR trains. Her job also required Audrey to have a good background knowledge of museums and galleries, cultural and scientific events, theatrical productions and a wide variety of 'factories or works specialising in a different industry'. She would certainly have needed a good set of research skills too. When a spokesman for the GWR summed her up however, he is

Miss Elizabeth 'May' Owen was on duty as stewardess on the SS *St Patrick*, on a regular run from Rosslare to Fishguard, when it was bombed and sunk in 1941 with many crew and passengers lost. For her incredible bravery at this time May was awarded the George Medal and the Lloyd's War Medal for Bravery at Sea.

quoted as saying: 'She is young and very charming. But she gets on well with other women all the same.' Did he, one wonders, realise what he was saying?

## Miss 'May' Owen

During the Second World War many railwaymen and women performed heroic deeds to keep the railways running and the people safe, that largely went unnoticed by Company, public, press or those who gave out official recognition. Happily, there were also many that performed outstanding deeds that did receive recognition. At the back of his book Collie Knox lists those who received 'Awards for Gallantry and Meritorious Service up to June 1944'. Among the ninety-seven listed as recommended by the Company and those recommended by outside authorities, are just two women:

> Mrs W.R.M. Crabbe Telephone Operator. Station: Swansea, Dept: Docks. Award: Commended.
> Miss E M. Owen Stewardess. Station: Fishguard Harbour. Dept: Docks. Award: GM, also awarded Lloyd's War Medal.

Miss Elizabeth May Owen, and Mrs Agnes Swayne were neighbours and good friends. They were both local girls of Goodwick near the port of Fishguard. They also both worked as stewardesses on the SS *St Patrick*, a cross-Channel steamer working between Rosslare and Fishguard. It was a job they both loved. For Agnes it had come as something of a lifesaver. Widowed at thirty with five small children she struggled for years to cope financially. Then came the offer of a post on the steamer, which seemed too good to be true. There was very little choice of employment for women and girls in the area and this job offered not only an interesting and varied life but financial security. While the onboard routine may have been the same each time, no crossing was the same. Agnes could not remember how many young mothers she had looked after or babies she had delivered. Both women were excellent sailors, they were never troubled with seasickness no matter how high or rolling the seas. There were usually two stewardesses on board, specifically assigned to help with the female passengers. On the eventful day, May had stood in for Agnes, who had been given compassionate leave because of the loss at sea of her first son, Oswald, who had been serving with the Merchant Navy. Also rostered was Mrs Jane Hughes, who was killed instantly and whose body was never recovered. The SS *St Patrick* had already taken two previous hits by enemy aircraft, but the third on Friday 13 June 1941 was to prove a hit too far: the ship, with her master, Captain J. Faraday, also the commodore captain of the GWR fleet, and his son Jack, as well as many crew and passengers, sank to the bottom of the sea. In all, eighteen crew members including Jane Hughes, lost their lives along with ten of the passengers.

The ship was some sixteen miles off Stumble Head in the early hours of the morning when the German bombers found her. The four bombs penetrated the cross bunker fuel tanks, which ran the breadth of the ship. The enormous explosion set the ship alight and killed many of the crew on or near the bridge and all bar one of the first-class passengers. The ship was severely damaged and started sinking at once, lasting only seven minutes. It was in dealing with the aftermath of the attack that May Owen displayed such bravery as to win not only the George Medal, the second highest civilian award for gallantry, but also the Lloyd's War Medal for Bravery at Sea. She was one of only two women to receive the Lloyd's Medal and the only woman on the staff of any railway company. Writing about the incident, Collie Knox says: 'When a woman finds herself in a situation in which bravery is called for she is apt to be very brave indeed.' Despite being, in the words of Mrs Betty Griffiths, who lived opposite her for a number of years, and whose husband was the marine superintendent at Fishguard, 'a nice but rather ordinary woman', May showed that, when she needed to be, she could be extraordinary or, to quote the *County Echo*, the local paper for Fishguard and Goodwick district, 'almost superhuman'.

There were twelve female passengers under May and Jane's charge, six women and one child in the top section and four women and a child in the bottom section. The explosion had broken the ship almost in two and put out all the electrics. The passengers below woke to confusion, mayhem and darkness. Jane Hughes was dead. The details of what May did next vary, but what is agreed is that her actions saved the lives of the women below deck. She made her way down gingerly in the darkness to the bottom section where her charges were. Here, to use Bernard Edwards words, she 'fought her way through the chaos'. The door leading to their quarters was jammed and the passengers trapped inside. May had to shoulder charge the door several times before she was able to get it open. By this time the ship was listing badly and the women and child were extremely frightened and a little hysterical. May managed to coax the passengers up the stairs clinging to each other. One of the women later commented, 'she coolly shepherded us on the deck'. When they arrived at the top of the stairs she had to then get them over to the port side because the emergency door was stuck. By now the fire was raging. Most of the lifeboats were lost in the flames, but one on the starboard side was being got away and May managed to get some of the women to it. The remaining passengers had then to be persuaded into the sea with their lifejackets on. Then May heard the frightened cries of a young woman, Dora O'Donaghue, a nurse who was returning to duty at Queen Charlotte's Hospital. Dora had fallen and hurt her side and had also lost her lifejacket. May went to help her. Dora told the reporters: 'the stewardess picked me up and told me, "there is no time to lose! Jump for your life".' So jump they did with Dora 'clinging tenaciously' to May. For almost two hours May

Mrs Agnes Swayne, a stewardess like her friend, neighbour and work colleague May Owen, was a local girl of Goodwick, near Fishguard. Agnes loved her job and did not want to retire. 'I never retired', she said. 'They retired me'

fought the sea, the oil slick and fought to keep the frightened, injured woman afloat. Eventually, covered in oil from the broken tanks, both women were hauled onto a raft and finally rescued by a lifeboat from the destroyer *Wolsey* Dora admitted to reporters that she 'owed her life to the calmness and resource of the stewardess'.

Agnes often wondered what would have happened if she had been on duty that day. She worried that, being of a different build to May, she may not have been able to get to the women down below. She very modestly said it was probably best that May had been there. Despite her dreadful ordeal, May continued to work as a stewardess on the ferries until she retired. She never married, choosing not to. Nor did Agnes marry again. Agnes said she never retired, they retired her! Betty, their young neighbour, remembers watching May and Agnes walking down the road, smart in their uniforms, chatting away on their way to work. 'Such kind ladies they were,' says Betty. 'Full of life. May was very modest. Never said a word about what she did. It was only other people who told me. She was very highly regarded.' When Agnes died many years after her retirement, her family were astonished to find not only the church 'filled to the gunnels' with custom officers and sailors of all titles, dressed in their best uniforms, but the whole route from the house to the church similarly lined. They were both, obviously, highly regarded and like the others written about, very distinctive women.[2]

1   All information from interviews with Dr B. Carter, *The Evening Advertiser* and the *Great Western Railway Magazine*.
2   The SS *St Patrick* was owned by the Fishguard & Rosslare Railways and Harbours Co. but came under the umbrella of the GWR's ferry services. All details on May Owen taken from Collie Knox's and Bernard Edward's books, the *GWR Magazine*. and *The County Echo*.

# CHAPTER 10

# AMONG THE STAFF

The in-house magazine was greatly favoured by railway companies as a means of conveying company policy, thinking and ethos to their employees. The *Great Western Railway Magazine*, originally owned by the Temperance Union but taken over by the GWR in 1903, was the first of its kind, and as a mouthpiece of the Company, makes fascinating reading. It is a social history document in its own right. As well as covering general important issues relating to the Company, such as wage negotiations, strikes and government legislation, it also reported on those specific to the GWR such as director appointments, traffic arrangements, company expansion and developments. It also always covered aspects of the staff welfare activities, especially the annual dinners and association gatherings.

A section entitled 'The Staff', reported on staff-related matters and listed changes, promotions and movements in the departments up and down the system. In later years this section became 'Among the Staff' and was freer in style and wider in content. Here, in very small articles, can be found all sorts of news items and announcements. For seekers of railwaywomen's history it is a wonderful resource as it offers rare insights, albeit in a limited fashion, into the working lives and glimpses of the personal lives of GWR's railwaywomen. One page in 1946 illustrates this fact, we can find information on types of jobs, 'Miss I. Mooney, a *fitter* in Slough shops, Road Motor Engineer's Department'; on length of service, 'Miss Bessie Flew of the CME's office has transferred to Newton Abbott after *thirty-five years* in the accounts office, Swindon'; on future prospects, 'Miss Phillis Brookes received a travelling valise from staff of the Goods Department, Newport, as a farewell gift on resigning from the service. Mr G. Halliday wished her success in *her new post with the Allied Military Control in Germany*'; as well as recognition of 'individual' achievements, 'Mrs Lily Hewer, a popular member of the clerical staff at the General Stores, Swindon, travelled daily from Purton and in twenty-eight-years service was invariably punctual with *an unbroken record of attendance* from 1921'. Over the years one also learns of women's promotions (rare), 'Miss C.A. Ault of the General Managers office has been appointed GWR Ambulance Centre Secretary' (1929) – and even deaths, that were quite frequent at times, 'Miss Lily Reynolds, a conductor in the Road Motor Car Department at Wolverhampton, passed away after a brief illness at Corwen, where she had been serving on relief duty. Miss Reynolds had been in the service since 1917. At the funeral the coffin, which was conveyed to Penn church in one of the Company's cars, was carried by six men of the staff' (1919). The GWR lost a number of their staff to 'the prevailing influenza

E.L. Winterton

# G.W.R.

Signal Engineer's Staff

∽ ∽

# Annual Outing to The Wye Valley

June 2nd, 1928.

# *Programme*

∽

| Reading | ... | ... | depart 8. 5 a.m. |
| Chepstow | ... | ... | arrive 11. 2 a.m. |

✢ ✢ ✢

## CHEPSTOW

| Luncheon on Train ... | ... | 12.15 p.m. |
| Depart by Char-a-bancs | ... | 1.30 p.m. |

✢ ✢ ✢

## TINTERN

| Arrive | ... | ... | ... | 2. 0 p.m. |
Visit Abbey—Sports.
| Depart | ... | ... | ... | 3.15 p.m. |

✢ ✢ ✢

## MONMOUTH

| Arrive | ... | ... | ... | 4. 0 p.m. |
| Depart | ... | ... | '... | 4.45 p.m. |
Return via Raglan and Usk to

| Newport | ... | ... | { arrive 6.40 p.m.<br>{ depart 6.58 p.m. |

Dinner will be served on train.

| Reading | ... | ... | arrive 8.56 p.m. |

*Above:* Office outings were very special occasions that were well planned and organised, as can be seen from this printed itinerary for a day's excursion to the Wye Valley in 1928.

*Right:* All girls together! The girls from the typing pool at Swindon Works on an office outing in 1928. Freda Denning (front row, first on the right) was the supervisor in charge of this office.

restaurants, and the opportunity was taken of presenting Mr. D. G. Kirk, of the Oswestry technical staff, with a case of fish knives and forks, to mark the occasion of his recent marriage. The presentation was made by Mr. R. C. Kirkpatrick.

On June 7, Mr. Norman Litten, a member of the divisional locomotive superintendent's staff at Worcester, on the occasion of his transfer to Swindon, was the recipient of a silver wristlet watch, subscribed for by the clerical staff. Mr. H. C. Rodda (divisional locomotive superintendent) made the presentation.

In the Conference Room of the Locomotive and Carriage Department, Newport, Mr. A. J. Pritchard was recently presented with an attaché case by Mr. E. G. Ireland, divisional locomotive superintendent, subscribed for by members of the office staff, to mark the occasion of his promotion as engine co-ordinator attached to the office of the locomotive superintendent at Swindon. Mr. Ireland referred to the ability of the recipient and of the esteem in which he was held by the whole staff. Mr. W. H. Roberts, chief clerk, and others also spoke.

Miss E. L. M. Whitehouse.    Miss E. M. Palmer

marrying a St. Dunstan's man, one of the early volunteers for active service, who joined up in September, 1914, and gained the Military Medal. Miss Whitehouse carries with her the good wishes of all the staff.

Miss EDITH M. PALMER, Newport, recently left the service of the Company on the occasion of her approaching marriage. She had been employed on the clerical staff of the Telegraph Department for eight and a-half years, the last seven and a-half of which had been spent at Newport (High Street) station. As a mark of esteem, her colleagues presented her with a dinner service. Miss Palmer is the daughter of the station master at Bassaleg.

A GATHERING took place, on June 5, at the Locomotive and Carriage accounts office, Swindon, when Miss E. Head was made the recipient of a silver tea service, as a mark of appreciation from her fellow clerks, on the occasion of her departure to Ontario and forthcoming marriage to Mr. H. L. Brust, formerly of the same office and now holding a responsible position in that city. Mr. J. Kelynack made the presentation.

Miss M. E. M. Brinded.    Miss O. M. Webb.

Miss M. E. M. BRINDED, of the Chief Engineer's office, Paddington, after 7½ years' service, has resigned in view of her approaching marriage. A presentation of a silver tea set was made to her by Mr. F. C. Warren, on behalf of her colleagues.

Miss OLIVE M. WEBB, of the Locomotive and Carriage Department accounts office at Swindon, who is shortly getting married, left the service on June 9, and received an oak dining table as a wedding gift from her colleagues. Mr. Kelynack, who made the presentation, said that Miss Webb entered the office a few days after war broke out in 1914 and was conspicuous for steady and efficient work.

Miss M. M. JAMES, who had been attached to the divisional superintendent's office at Pontypool Road since 1913, resigned on May 19 to be married. Before leaving, Mr. Cox (chief clerk) handed her, on behalf of the office staff, an appropriate gift, as a token of their esteem.

Miss E. L. M. WHITEHOUSE, of Paddington goods office, was the recipient of a pretty 54-piece dinner service from the clerical staff, on resigning from the service on the occasion of her approaching marriage. In addition to her ordinary office duties, Miss Whitehouse did most excellent work during the air raids, especially among the women porters working in the Paddington goods shed during the war. She also devoted her spare time to V.A.D. work at St. Dunstan's Hospital, and is

A PRESENTATION was recently made to Miss A. Mills, of the Bristol divisional superintendent's office, who had recently left the Company's service to be married. On behalf of the staff of the office, where Miss Mills had been employed for over seven years, Mr. H. Griffiths, divisional superintendent, presented her with an eight-day oak striking clock, an oak biscuit box and a marmalade pot.

Miss E. Head.    Miss A. R. Mills

This page is taken from the GWR's in-house magazine, 1923, and gives a wonderful insight into the roles of women within the company.

epidemic' at this time, and there are many recorded deaths of young women, which, from their tone, suggests the GWR found a difficult burden to bear.

Whilst women's arrival in post were rarely announced, apart from a handful of 'firsts', like first messenger girl, and, of course, the photographs announcing their arrival as war recruits, their departures often did appear, 'Miss Gracie Hearn, who entered the Divisional Superintendents Office, Paddington in May 1913 as the first woman clerk, resigned in October 1916 to take up other employment'; this was especially so when they were leaving to be married. This was the reason that Miss Hamilton, the first female supervisor in the telegraph office in 1908, made it on to the magazine pages in 1915. At the same time as we learn of Miss Hamilton, we are also told of the departure of Miss F.E. Daw, who had been the supervisor in the Birmingham telegraph office since 9 January 1911 and who was also leaving to be married. This was the beginning of a new editorial trend, a new 'item of interest', that was, happily for the mainly male readership, often accompanied by a fetching photograph. During the 1920s it would quite often happen that almost a whole page of the edition would be given up to such marriage notices and photographs.

Miss Hamilton's marriage was part of another new GWR trend, finding one's husband or wife at work. She found and married a Mr Goatley, one of the telegraph operators at Paddington. Such was the enthusiasm for this trend by their employees, that it is remarked upon in the *Magazine* in 1924 in a somewhat overwhelmed tone:

> The list of GWR clerks who, finding the proximity of lady clerks so congenial and their assistance so helpful, decide to take them as partners for life, is steadily growing. This applies to a marked degree to the Swindon Locomotive, Carriage and Wagon Department accounts staff. A number of such romances have already been recorded … and we now have to announce others.

It then goes on to identify the latest women, who they married, who made the presentations of gifts, what they received and when they left:

> Miss Dorothy E. Gale, left 9 August, married Mr H.D. Miles, received a handsome dinner service presented by Mr F. Bailey, also Miss D.J. Ballinger, left 6 September, married Mr D.H. Sheward, received an extending leaf dining table in dark oak, presented by Mr H.R. Goudge.

It would appear that this practice quickly spread along the line as in 1925 the *Magazine* writes 'an epidemic of marriages has occurred among members of the staff at Pearson Place, Cardiff'.

The generosity of the wedding gifts from their work colleagues stands out, especially considering the generally low level of wages paid. Solid-oak sideboard, extending oak table, gate-leg table, sofas and easy chairs, walnut hall stand, a canteen of stainless steel cutlery, or a handsome dinner service are often mentioned amongst the larger items during the 1920s. Smaller items mentioned are a silver-mounted pickle jar, silver teapot with inscription, handsome clock with Westminster chimes, a sardine server and crumb scoop, hearthrug, some cut-glass vases, a carver set, an eiderdown and, several times, 'a wallet of treasury notes'; these smaller items were more likely to be given in the difficult 1930s. All gifts came from collections made amongst colleagues. One of the more intriguing collections made is that for Miss Stevens, a booking clerk at Henley-in-Arden station, who was to marry Mr J. Harrison, the leading porter. Their gift, a clock, was subscribed to by 'members of the travelling public, tradesmen and the staff'. Obviously they were a popular couple! These marriage notices continued through the 1930s although gradually getting less frequent, and with the photographs beginning to be omitted. The outbreak of the Second World War turned minds to more serious matters and in the 1940s women were on the pages in relation to their wartime roles.

Working for the GWR meant fun in out-of-office-hours activities run through the Social & Education Union – later the Staff Association. Young women got to participate in sports that would otherwise not have been available to them. Hockey, football, swimming, athletics were all options. This is the GWR hockey team of February 1918. Front row: first left, Ella Winterton who loved to play in goal. Middle row: first left, Elsie Winterton. Top row: far right, Miss Day.

Throughout the years many articles and photographs appear in relation to the activities of various clubs and branches of the Social and Education Union, later to become the Staff Association. These activities and clubs offered wonderful opportunities for self development, creative leisure and companionship, as well as escape from family chores. For those who enjoyed sports there was a host of things to choose from: swimming, running, athletics, tennis, football for men and women. You could be very fit with the GWR. Music was a central part of many clubs whether as bands, choirs, individual singing competitions or even performing opera. For those more cerebrally inclined there were debating societies, chess, the literary society and the library. Reports on any of these could be regularly found in each *Magazine* edition.

Sometimes one can find women on the more general pages, usually within articles about some specific department. Here one comes across more treasures as in 'the Learned Ladies of London' in the central enquiries office, Paddington, or Miss Emma Saunders, the 'Railwayman's Friend', or Miss Jose Potier, the Belgian refugee in the First World War. Miss Potier's father had left Antwerp amidst a full-scale bombardment leaving his family, Jose, her mother and two sisters behind. Several days later they followed him. They then had a 'trying journey to the frontier' made worse by the wintry weather. After days spent 'waiting for a favourable opportunity for crossing … the family crawled through the barbed wire at great risk of being observed and shot' and finally escaped through the German lines into Holland. They still faced a harrowing journey with heavy rains and snow to reach Flushing from where, after much delay and difficulty, they

Barry Docks Ladies Team – GWR Ladies Football Cup Winners 1946. Front row, left to right: B. Oram; P. Jones; P. James; P. Hamilton (captain); V. Booker; W. James; J. Turner. Second row, left to right: Mr H.R. Bate (chairman); D. Williams; E. Dowdeswell; E. Sheppard; M. Owen (vice-captain); B. McCarthy; Mr T. Carpenter (president). Back row, left to right: Mr G. Foley (coach); Mr F.S. Baldwin (general secretary); Mr I.T. David (vice-chairman).

managed to get to England. Fortunately for them, their plight then came to the notice of Miss Jaffray of Skilts, Redditch, who found them a cottage and got Jose a 'trial' in the booking office at Birmingham under the benevolent eye of Mr S.F. Johnson, the divisional superintendent. Luckily, Jose 'proved herself an intelligent and quick pupil who spoke English like a native'. In 1916 Her Imperial and Royal Highness Princess Napoleon, daughter of the late King Leopold of Belgium, was officially visiting Birmingham to open an exhibition of art by Belgian artists. Jose was brought forward and presented to the Princess at Snow Hill station. It was a very extraordinary story, exciting and daring and read like a 'boy's-own adventure'!

One aspect that is generously covered in the *Magazine* is that of staff retirements. Several women who, having remained single, had long careers with the GWR and are thus acknowledged, such as Miss Cann and Miss Holder who were in 'housekeeping'. It was never going to be easy for women to carve a career in the railway industry, but one area where their abilities were found necessary and desirable was in 'domestic service' where they could use their 'womanly skills' of cleaning, cooking and housekeeping. The railway refreshment rooms was the first big opportunity in this respect. In his book, commonly known as *Stokers and Pokers* of 1849, Sir Francis Head, a social observer of the day, wrote a spirited description of the Wolverhampton refreshment room. In it he describes the activities of 'seven young ladies' who rise 'exactly at seven to be ready and waiting to receive the passengers off the first train of the day', which reaches Wolverhampton at 7.30 a.m.

Escaping from war-torn Belgium during the First World War, Jose Potier's story reads like a boy's-own-adventure but she was happy to end up working for the GWR in their booking office at Birmingham station.

The GWR had large refreshment rooms at Paddington, Swindon and Bristol, as well as at other main stations along its system, and from the *Magazine* we learn of two ladies who made a career working in these places. Miss Florence H. Cann had been manageress of the refreshment rooms at Paddington. She had commenced her railway career at Bristol in 1883. During the thirty-one years she spent with the refreshment rooms department she worked in Weston-super-Mare, Newton Abbot, and Oxford before taking up her final position at Paddington in 1899. It must have been an exciting time for Florence, travelling up and down the country to improve her position. She must have been a woman of great independence and spirit, competent and able to look out for herself. The face that looks out from her small photograph looks confident and assured, the face of someone who is at ease with themselves. She retired from the Company's service in 1914. It would have been lovely to have heard some of Florence's reflections on things that happened over these three decades. Whilst we do not have that opportunity with Florence, twenty-one years later, we do get it with Miss F.M. Holder when she retired in 1935.

Miss F.M. Holder, described in the *GWR Magazine* as 'one of the best-known railway personalities in the west of England', retired from the Company's service on 31 May 1935. It is such as shame that whilst acknowledging the impact of her 'personality' the GWR did not also acknowledge her first name! She had worked in the refreshment rooms at Bristol Temple Meads station since March 1886 and had progressed 'through all branches of the business to become manageress', a position she held when the GWR took over the establishment from the tenant in 1914. On her retirement she had clocked up nearly fifty years of service and seen a great many changes in the role of the railways in peoples lives and in the status and place of women in society. Looking at their work records, it may well have been that Florence and Miss Holder worked together in Bristol, even for a short time.

Miss Holder is given the opportunity to 'pen a few notes of her reminiscences' for the magazine. It is an opportunity given to very few women so it is disappointing that she did not take this chance to give us a 'personal' voice or describe in detail her own working life. Instead what we do get is some intriguing insights into the changing times of the station and railways. Miss Holder lived through exciting times for the railways such as the 'Battle of the Gauges' and had seen and experienced first hand the complications of trying to run two such systems. Passengers arriving at Bristol from London, Devon or Cornwall would arrive on GWR broad-gauge trains but should they wish to travel to the North or to South Wales they had to change onto 'narrow-gauge trains' (now called standard gauge). During the changeover passengers took the chance to visit the refreshment rooms and, says Miss Holder, 'when excursions were run, it made us very busy'. That seems to be a remarkable understatement. Being at one station for so many years Miss Holder was able to document not only the changes in railway practices, but also those in social customs. She writes of these which also give us some small indications as to her work:

> The new station at Temple Meads is a much larger concern than the one I started in… The work in the refreshment rooms has altered considerably in recent years. The introduction of dining cars did away with the very hurried serving of meals to passengers while waiting for their train to leave. The number of luncheon baskets that had to be prepared for the express trains was very great and it was often difficult to satisfy the requirements of the various customers. The greater number of trains that now run spread the work more evenly throughout the day, so that we do not have the really terrific rushes that used to occur on the arrival of one long heavy train. People do not require such heavy meals now as years ago, and they judge more by quality than quantity.

Miss Holder had worked at the station through the First World War and she recalls that when dealing with the troop trains: 'It was not unusual to have to provide hundreds of mugs of beer, as well as bread and cheese, in about ten minutes.' What a masterpiece of management that must have been. Miss Holder appears to have enjoyed her long working life and is sad to be leaving. She writes: 'It is naturally with much regret that I am leaving the old scenes. I shall be taking into my retirement the very pleasant recollections of the old station and of those with whom I was associated there for so many years.'

What is perhaps surprising to find in these notices, given the Company's previously studious reluctance to acknowledge the potential benefits of female employees is the mainly warm, appreciative and even congratulatory way they write of the women, albeit in the manner of a paternal, elderly uncle. At the presentation to Mrs Bennett, leaving to rejoin her husband, and Miss Wolf, whose wedding was approaching, it is remarked: 'both young women were much liked and their colleagues were sorry to lose them'. Presenting Miss S. May with a silver toilet set on her forthcoming marriage in 1925, Mr W.N. Thompson, the Cardiff Docks superintendent, referred to 'the excellent manner in which Miss May's duties had been carried out'. Of Miss E. Binham at the office of the Bristol divisional superintendent, reference was made to her 'many good qualities and her success in the signalling and station accountancy examinations', while in regard to Miss Mooney, the fitter in the Slough shops, Mr G. Weaver spoke of 'her efficiency and sunny disposition and voiced the united good wishes of the donors for her future happiness'. All of this was generous and wholesome praise that could as easily have been left out. Many are given fulsome recognition for their work and attainments as they are waved 'goodbye', Miss Holder, Miss Cann, Miss Ault, Miss Thing and Miss Sturgeon are but a few. Here are just three as taken from the *Magazine*:

> Miss C Ault, GWR Ambulance Centre Secretary retires on 3 October after thirty-years service with the Company, during twenty-six of which she has been a member of the general manager's staff. For upwards of a quarter of a century, Miss Ault has been connected with the GWR ambulance movement. During the last war when her predecessor, Mr W.G. Chapman, was ambulance secretary, she took over his duties for the four years he was serving with the Forces and upon his return acted as his assistant, until July 1929 when she was promoted ambulance centre secretary. During her period of office the movement reached its zenith when in 1939 no fewer than 9,973 members of the staff passed examinations in first aid.
>
> Her success has been largely due to high administrative abilities, coupled with a kindly and unobtrusive zeal for the cause she served, and an ability to infect others with her enthusiasm.

During her centre secretaryship, Miss Ault has been a member of headquarters committees of the Order of St John and her work was specially recognised in 1929 by admission to the Order as a serving sister.

Miss Ault has many outside interests and with her new leisure will doubtless exercise her literary talent, having already had three books published.

The many friends she has made throughout the system will wish Miss Ault health and happiness in full measure during many years of retirement.

For services rendered:

Throughout the war, Reading goods staff had sent comforts to their colleagues and relatives serving with the Forces. It was Miss Irene Thing, who in December 1939 organised the 'penny-a-week' fund which financed the effort. Under her guidance the scheme expanded to include donations to special war appeals and the adoption of the minesweeper, *Neil Smith*. Clear evidence of her success was given by the balance sheet issued at the closing down of the fund: in six years Miss Thing had collected £609. Over 80,000 cigarettes, 150 pipes, 300 pairs of socks and nearly 100 pullovers were amongst the gifts despatched, and – an act which meant much to those away from home – Miss Thing personally wrote 2,000 letters to the men in all parts of the world. Among other causes which benefited were St Dunstan's, the Red Cross and St John and the Malta Relief Fund. Wishing to show in some striking way their appreciation, contributors to the fund decided to present her with an illuminated address, signed by every member. Mr H.S. Veltom, goods agent, made the presentation and praised her loyalty and unremitting efforts.

*Left:* First aid and St John's Ambulance played a major part in peoples' work lives on the GWR. A great deal of emphasis was placed on it. Many classes, competitions and annual prize-givings took place and were regularly reported in the *Magazine*.

*Opposite:* Firefighting was serious business at any time on the railways but especially during the Second World War and the Blitz. There were a number of women's teams of firefighters all over the GWR system and they would compete against each other just to be 'the best'. Regular fire drill and firefighting practice could become tedious but these competitions added fun and pride in the work and made sure everyone was fully prepared and up to scratch should such an event arise.

Accepting the gift Miss Thing said what keen pleasure the effort to brighten the lives of the fighting men had given.

Finally:

Miss Alice A Sturgeon of the statistical mileage staff, chief mechanical engineer's department, Swindon, has retired after nearly thirty-one-years of service. A gold medallist of the St John Ambulance Association, Miss Sturgeon also holds a long-service award of the St John Ambulance Brigade. She was presented with a sum in treasury notes by Mr H.G. Lewis, clerk-in-charge of the statistical section, who on behalf of colleagues and friends 'wished her health and happiness in her retirement'. Other speakers praised Miss Sturgeon's friendly and cooperative ways and said how much her presence would be missed.

These railway 'career' women appeared to have led very fulfilled and interesting lives. What stands out in their stories is the dedication that they gave to service, both in their jobs and in the activities they championed. What also comes through are the benefits that accrue to the Company, the staff and the women.

The GWR's relationship with its female employees is intriguing. That it was problematical for the Company on many levels is unmistakable but that they were caring in an authoritative, paternalistic way is also evident. Their changing relationship and attitudes towards the women can be seen through the pages of the *Magazine*. Although the GWR gradually learns to treat the women as grown-ups rather than 'the weaker sex', it never quite casts off the mantle of grand gentleman in *loco parentis* towards '*the fair sex*'.

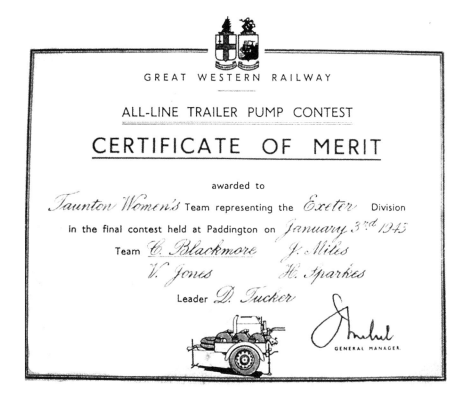

Firefighting competitions looked very dramatic and were great fun but were also hard work with a serious reason.

The winning team: ladies of Paddington goods depot at Bristol parcels depot take the handsome shield, which had been provided by General Manager Sir James Milne, for the trailer pump trials in September 1944. As many as twelve women's teams would have entered.

# Abbreviations and Terms

AEU    Amalgamated Engineers Union
BTC    British Transport Commission
CME    Chief Mechanical Engineer
MRC    Modern Record Office, Warwick
NUR    National Union of Railwaymen
PRO    Public Record Office, Kew
RCA    Railway Clerks' Association
REC    Railway Executive Committee

Check: Each GWR employee had their own 'check', a little metal disc with their Works' number on. This was put on a check board each morning and had to be taken off by the employee as they came in. Remaining checks indicated who was not at work.

Feminised: a term applied to work such as typing or which had started out as men's work but had become an occupation principally for women.

The *Magazine*: The GWR's own in-house magazine.

Memorial: Equivalent to today's petitions.

# Sources and Bibliography

## Interviews and Records

*Great Western Magazine*, GWR Minute Books, GWR Circulars & Reports; at STEAM Museum of the Great Western Railway, Swindon Reference Library and private collections.

Rosa Matheson's Doctorate Thesis, 'Women and the Great Western Railway, with Special Reference to Swindon Works', and all sources therein.

Hunt, N. (1987), *Memories of the Old Great Western Railway – A Lifetime Recollection from a Woman's Point of View*, STEAM Museum of the Great Western Railway, Swindon.

GWR Staff Committee Minute Books 1909–1937, GWR Trust, Didcot Railway Centre.

NPR 2/ – Staff registers and documents, Chester Record Office, Chester.

GWR Staff Records, Local History Archive, Trowbridge Reference Library.

Photographs: Private and family collections, STEAM Museum of the Great Western Railway and Special Collections, University of Leicester Library.

The Fawcett Library Press Cuttings on Women and Railways 1939–60.

## Books

Bryan, T. (1995), *The Great Western at War 1939–1945*, Patrick Stephens Ltd.

Cohn, S. (1985), *The Process of Occupational Sex-typing: The Feminisation of Clerical Labour in Britain*, Temple University Press.

Cook, K.J. (1974), *Swindon Steam 1921–1951*, Ian Allan Ltd.

Darwin, B. (1946), War *on the Line: The Story of the Southern Railway in Wartime*, The Southern Railway Company.

Drummond, D.R. (1995), *Crewe: Railway Town, Company and People – 1840–1914*, Scholar Press.

Head, Sir Francis (1849), *Stokers and Pokers*.

Knox, C. (1944), *The Unbeaten Track*, Cassell &. Co. Ltd.

Lewis, J. (1984), *Women in England 1870–1950*, Wheatsheaf Books.

Peck, A.S. (1983), *The Great Western at Swindon Works*, Oxford Publishing Co.

Pratt, E. (1921), *War Record of the Great Western Railway*, Selwyn & Blount Ltd.

Priddle, R. and Hyde, D. (1996), *GWR to Devizes*, Millstream Books.

Marwick, A. (1977), *Women at War 1914–1918*, Fontana Books.

Nock, O.S. (1971), *Britain's Railways At War 1939–1945*, Ian Allan Ltd.

Russell, J.K.L. (1983), *GWR Company Servants*, Wild Swan Publications.

Searle, M.V. (1986), *Down the Line to Bristol*, Bloomsbury Books.

Simmons, J. & Biddle, G., eds, *The Oxford Companion to British Railway History*, Oxford University Press.

Summerfield, P. (1998), *Reconstructing Women's Wartime Lives*, Manchester University Press.

Tomkins, R. & Sheldon, P. (1990), *Swindon and the GWR*, Alan Sutton & Redbrick.

Vaughan, A. (1973), *A Pictorial Record of Great Western Signalling*.

Wallace, M. (1996), *Single or Return? The History of the Transport Salaried Staff Association*, TSSA.

Williams, A. (1915) *Life in a Railway Factory*, Duckworth & Co.

Great Western Railway Centenary Number of *The Times* (1972), *Great Western Progress 1835–1935*, David & Charles Rubs Ltd.

## Journals and Newspapers

Smith, Harold L. (1984), 'The Historical Journal', 27.4, *The Manpower Problem in Britain During The Second World War*, pp.925–45

*The Chronicle & Cheshire, North Wales Advertiser*

*The County Echo*

*The Daily Chronicle*

*The Daily Herald*

*The Daily Telegraph*

*The Great Western Railway Magazine*

*The News Chronicle*

*The Railway Gazette*

*The Railway Magazine*

*The Railway Sheet and Official Gazette*

*The Evening Advertiser*

*The Swindon Advertiser*

# Other titles published by Tempus

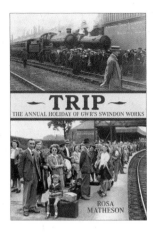

## TRIP The Annual Holiday of GWR's Swindon Works
ROSA MATHESON

This book provides an evocative record of Trip for those who remember the excursions and for anyone interested in the history of Swindon and the administrative prowess of the GWR. Archive photographs and postcards offer a fascinating glimpse of Swindon Works and the families on holiday at an array of Trip destinations.

978 0 7524 3909 9

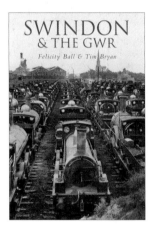

## Swindon & the GWR
FELICITY BALL & TIM BRYAN

This book features rare and unpublished pictures of men and women who worked at Swindon, from the collection of images at STEAM: Museum of the Great Western Railway. Inluded in these pages are GWR locomotives, royal visits, staff outings and the famous TRIP holiday, showing a glimpse of life beyond the factory walls.

978 0 7524 2801 7

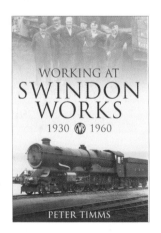

## Working for Swindon Works 1930–1960
PETER TIMMS

This is a fascinating and important record of the day to day conditions faced by the many thousands of working men and women and their families whose lives were controlled by the GWR from 1930–1960, the beginning of the modern period for the railway with mechanical accounting, up to the decline of the railway from 1957. This book includes many previously unpublished pictures.

978 0 7524 4403 1

If you are interested in purchasing other books published by Tempus, or in case you have difficulty finding any Tempus books in your local bookshop, you can also place orders directly through our website

www.tempus-publishing.com